Nabonidus
and the
Queen
of
Sheba

Nabonidus and the Queen of Sheba

Roots of a Legend

JANET TYSON

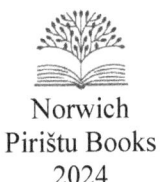

Norwich
Prištu Books
2024

Copyright © 2024 by Janet Tyson. All rights reserved. This book may not be reproduced, in whole or in part, in any form, without written permission from the publisher.

Cover: Author's own photograph and editing.

British Library Cataloguing in Production Data. A catalogue record for this book is available from the British Library.

ISBN: 978-1-7393154-7-4

Contents

Preface   i

Seba   1
The Cushite, the drunkard, and the Elixir

Geographical Sheba   17
"Sheba and Dedan"

Keturah   32
A metaphorical true-love

Hatshepsut   52
A role model for us, not them

Ethiopia & Islam   61
Kebra Nagast and Islamic lore

Demon   77
Hairy legged bloodsucker

Poetic License   95
"Queen of the south," a Tayma legend, and a "lovers' Wind"

Thoughts   115

Appendix   119

Bibliography   121

Index   127

Preface

THIS BOOK IS THE THIRD IN A series of investigations into the last King of Babylon, Nabonidus (556-539 BCE) and his significance to the early Jews. The work began with an investigation into the potential historical roots of the Song of Solomon, which I claimed to be a first-hand account of the stormy marriage between Nabonidus and his exotic Egyptian bride, Nitocris II, First Prophet of Amun and daughter of Ahmose III.[1] The resulting insights led seamlessly into the exodus narratives, which I have assessed as being the chronicles of the initial 'exodus' of the Jews *from Babylonia* after the Edict of Cyrus of 539 BCE; Nabonidus led them.[2]

These two academic investigations provide the basis for much of what will be discussed here, so I would suggest at least the book on the Song of Solomon be downloaded and kept as a reference, for I will be citing the pages of relevant material as we go along, rather than bulk out this edition with repetition. Familiarity with the new

---

[1] Janet Tyson, *She Brought the Art of Women: A Song of Solomon, Nabonidus, and the Goddess* (Norwich: Pirištu Books, 2023). Available for download online.

[2] Janet Tyson, *Arabian Sinai: Nabonidus and the Exodus* (Norwich: Pirištu Books, 2024).

paradigm I have set out, which places Nabonidus and Nitocris at the very core of much of the Hebrew Bible (HB), will make my reasoning clearer. This is not an exercise in further romanticising the familiar "Queen of Sheba"; this is an *alternative* perception of the details and etymological patterns that form the foundation, the roots, of her legend. These may not be what you expect, and my theories are still being honed, but I think you will find at least one of these seven discussions will ignite your curiosity.

I aim to demonstrate how even this allegedly mysterious and apparently floating legend of the Queen of Sheba can find rationalisation and consistent meaning *in situ*, if the roots of the legend are sought in the Nabonidus/Nitocris relationship and its aftermath. Even the much later, more fanciful, augmented tales of Ethiopian and Islamic lore contain elements that have strong correlations in a 6th Century BCE context.

The Song's depiction of the couple is far from the romantic love affair tradition has spoon-fed us; it is dark, at times violent, and it deals with subjects the average commentary dare not discuss. Nitocris is branded a troublemaker, a clingy, jealous, loose-cannon in the king's court, a foreigner, a sorceress, a powerful but "despised" woman.

From what I could discern, Nitocris died very soon after the invasion of Babylon in 539 BCE, having spent the previous four years serving as the *entu*[3] (regent) at the temple of Sîn at Ur. Her ghost, however, was to haunt the first Jews to leave Babylonia under the Edict of Cyrus, for she became a key figure in the tales of Abraham in Genesis, i.e., she became the character "Sarah." Once again, much research went into discovering this subtext,

---

[3] The high priestess of an all-female priesthood revived by Nabonidus after centuries of being defunct.

Preface

and it proved consistent with the perspective noted in the Song. Nitocris was *still* the focus of blame, of angst; in effect, she became a scapegoat.

The account of Nabonidus' marriage to Nitocris was probably initiated during the four-year stay at Ur and augmented for a few years afterward, by the woman who knew the couple intimately, Jehudijah. She was Nabonidus' second-wife, i.e., in status somewhere between wife and concubine, and was on the exodus with Nabonidus, so the continuation of an interest in Nitocris, even after her death, might well have been due to Jehudijah's continued resentment of her nemesis during the exodus. The treatment of "Sarah" is intentionally catty, mean-spirited, and harsh, as if a score is being settled; parts of Genesis might well have been written, or at least influenced by Jehudijah's supporters (Jehudijah herself died on the exodus); it is evident from this statement that I argue for a later-than-Exodus date for the Genesis composition. The Genesis genealogies, especially, substantiate my claim, as you will see.[4]

I am convinced the Queen of Sheba is based on, or inspired by, the same Nitocris that appears in the Song of Solomon, served at Ur, and was vilified by Jehudijah and the early Jews as Solomon's Egyptian wife. I am also certain that the epithet is purely symbolic, contains both personal and geographical meaning, and that her introduction in 1 Kings 10 has been greatly misconstrued.

---

[4] See also my related papers on www.academia.edu.

1

Seba

IT HAS BECOME EVIDENT TO me that the Genesis genealogies serve as a legend, as on a map, providing the reader with signposts to the narratives that follow, i.e., the exodus narratives. The only thing is, you can't really see this until you already understand the narratives as contemporaneous accounts of Nabonidus' return to Tayma, via Canaan, after the fall of Babylon (in 539 BCE). There are positive memories of this event, written by those who seem to have got what they wanted out of their escape from bondage as exiles (i.e., those who were taken to Canaan and remained there) but the bulk of the exodus narrative is very dark, sombre, and negative.

The authors of Genesis were a later generation; they understood the recent history of their parents, or grandparents, and they created the lineages and the brilliantly thought-out names, to produce this legend for future generations. The genealogies *anticipate* the Moses stories and provide a sort of preordainment, suggesting everything that happened, as bad as it was for those first returnees from Babylon (though many had never been to Canaan, being born in Babylonia), was inevitable and just one of God's divine tools for the refinement of the Jewish people. It was all meant to be.

In these genealogies, there are three "sons" called "Sheba": of Raamah, son of Cush (Gen 10:7); of Joktan, brother of Peleg (Gen 10:28); and of Jokshan, son of Abraham and Keturah (Gen 25:2). Starting the legend is "Seba," the offspring of Cush. This "Seba" represents, I contend, Nitocris II.

"Cush" is a name that is attested beyond the HB. The ancient Egyptians called Upper Nubia "Cush" since about 2500 BCE and most translators and commentators suggest it simply means "dark" or "black." The 25th Dynasty Cushite "black pharaohs" ruled Egypt from 747-656 BCE and I suggest it is for this very reason Nitocris is referred to as the "Cushite woman" (Num 12:1); she was black, royal, and Egyptian, though she hailed from the Libyan dynasty of Necho II.[1] I have argued that linking her to Libya would have identified her in the HB texts and this was consistently avoided, as both her and Nabonidus' names were anathema to the postexilic Jews. This is why there are so many different pseudonyms, i.e., "commission names" (as I call them) that provide new information in each distinct context, yet still relate back to the respective (historical) character, etymologically.[2]

In Gen 10:7, "Seba" is figuratively the firstborn of Cush and "Sheba" is the firstborn of Raamah. The position of firstborn is profoundly significant in the HB, for it signifies heredity, primacy, etc., yet the only one of these 'sons of Cush' to be given further attention, in terms of lineage, is Raamah, the fourth of the five sons. The firstborn of Cush, "Seba," is conspicuously ignored in

---

[1] Tyson, *She Brought*, 21-2.
[2] Tyson, *Arabian Sinai*, Appendix 5, "Primary Commission Names," 385-6.

terms of descendants.

For "son" the Hebrew uses *ben* but in the plural this can include a group of people, male and female (not always related biologically). There is at least one female in the HB who is presented in a masculine context, e.g., Sophereth (Neh 7:57) or Hassophereth (Ezra 2:55), "the female scribe"; she is so camouflaged by the males surrounding her in the text, she wasn't really (openly) noticed for centuries. I suggest "Seba" is another example, purposefully hiding the tale of Nitocris (who is a major player in the entire story of Nabonidus and his eventual role as "Moses") beneath a veneer of masculinity.

The name "Seba" means something like "one who drinks," i.e., something that intoxicates, from the verb *saba'*, "to imbibe." The noun *saba* means "drunkard." Intriguingly, Abarim Publications suggests there is "something secretive about this name," claiming that most biblical dictionaries avoid interpreting it, or simply suggest "Eminent."[3] This is fascinating, as my very first thought, coming from my recent interpretation of the Song of Solomon and the exodus narratives, is that this hints at the most controversial but sustained and (I think) undeniable aspect of the Nabonidus-Nitocris legends, i.e., the imbibing of the Elixir Rubeus.

The Elixir Rubeus was a highly secretive and sacred rite performed by the pharaohs and their high priests, involving the drinking of female menstrual blood and male semen. It was said to make the imbiber "one with the gods" in that it was hallucinogenic, containing, it is thought, various botanical ingredients that were known to have psychedelic properties. It is referred to as the "cup of abominations" in Rev 17:4.[4] Very little is said of this rite outside esoteric investigations, but the Song depicts it

---

[3] "Seba," Abarim Publications, https://www.abarim-publications.com.

[4] Tyson, *She Brought*, 31-4. 95-7, et al.

quite clearly, and even tells of Nabonidus' addiction to it, and how he brought it from Tayma to Babylon on his return in 543 BCE. It's all 'between the lines'; I did not go in search of this information and I knew nothing of the Elixir before uncovering it in the Song and researching the details of what appeared to me to be an arcane ritual.

Nitocris II, Nabonidus' conciliatory bride, was not just Ahmose III's daughter, she was also First Prophet of Amun and, so I have suggested, also either a God's Wife and/or God's Hand. In this latter capacity, she would have been responsible for the Elixir, for protecting the young temple women who would supply the blood for the rite.[5] She seems to have loved her role, so the Song infers. When it came time for her to breed, i.e., the expectation of Nabonidus for a daughter to dedicate to his favourite lunar deity Sîn putting her under pressure to do so, she rebelled by purposely aborting her foetus. She wished to maintain the sanctity of her womb-blood (i.e., "wine," for the Elixir) and so, like Scheherazade (another fable I think is based on Nitocris), she attempted to keep Nabonidus at bay, first by offering him insights into her mystical religion (which led to the tales of Solomon's search for wisdom, but also as one who delved into his wives' religions). This he loved, but he was not a good student, being easily distracted, and when he began to lose his patience

Figure 1: Nitocris was the guardian of the Elixir Rubeus, the most secret and ancient rite of Pharaohs (Image: Author's photo)

---

[5] Tyson, *She Brought*, 55.

with Nitocris, she feigned another pregnancy to keep him from expelling her as Queen (or worse).

Meanwhile, the Elixir had become a bad habit for the king, to the point of him holding debauched parties of "friends" who would visit him at court for a taste of this magical potion. The Song of Solomon ends with an acerbic remark about how he charged men a hefty price to experience this ancient, highly sexual, Egyptian rite. Subsequently, in the tales of the exodus, Nabonidus is depicted as still being addicted to this concoction, trying to procure it, and being forced to face up to his unsavoury antics. The association of Nitocris' blood is very strong in the HB and is, in Genesis, included in the very first named descendant of "Cush": "Seba." Much of the tale of Moses rests on this foundation, on this precursor, so the literary construct of a genealogy is fitting.

If Nitocris was known to be at the centre of this blood-habit of the king's, it would be logical for her, i.e., the Queen, to be referred to as the Queen of Seba, or the Queen of Imbibing (the intoxicating Elixir). That is, although she, herself, did not imbibe she was the symbolic fountain/well of womb-blood, she was in charge of all the other ladies who served in this capacity, and she was the one with the knowledge of how to create the Elixir, its associated secret rites, and its effects.[6]

Perhaps even more apropos, the verb *saba*, in Arabic, means "to pour, or to flow," and it is also a noun meaning "discharge"; this more aptly refers to Nitocris' menstrual blood, the main ingredient of the Elixir.

This Elixir might seem rather obscure and eccentric today, as we have not had reason to consider this aspect of the Song of Solomon, Nabonidus, or Moses, before; the more I research, the more I am convinced this is a strong but well-hidden subtext. It is a basis for the mysticism and arcane symbolism of the Song and the judgement imposed

---

[6] Tyson, *She Brought*, 54-5.

upon Nabonidus by the early Jewish priests/authors.

Notably, the Egyptian word *sba* means "star," and *sbayt* means "instruction of wisdom guiding to the right path."[7] The goddess Ishtar, the prime avatar of Nitocris in the Song of Solomon, is represented by a star; and Nitocris, as First Prophet of Amun, *attempts* to teach Nabonidus (as Solomon) the ancient wisdom of her Osirian faith and the ethical and moral principles of *maat*.

When Nitocris is alluded to in the HB, however, either directly or as an abstract notion of feminine immorality, etc., she is the focus of disdain, ridicule, and deeply rooted fear. The Queen of Sheba, or rather, the Queen of Seba (i.e., with the "s" sound of Arabic, rather than the "sh" of Hebrew), needs to be approached with this in mind.

Initiation?

In *She Brought*, I discuss a certain 3rd Century CE Gnostic Egyptian cult that apparently arose as a direct consequence of a specific perspective on the Song of Solomon.[8] They were called the Phibionites, and they seized upon the more arcane and esoteric aspects of the Elixir rite and Nitocris' sacerdotal role in the Song, following her example (literally) religiously.

In a similar vein, perhaps, there is a mysterious sect in the Quran called the Sabians (2:62; 5:69; 22:17). There has been much speculation concerning their identity and practices, but no consensus. What is claimed is that they were a chimeric sect, absorbing elements of Judaism, Christianity, and even Zoroastrianism; they were thought to be Chaldeans and therefore linked to Abraham (who is

---

[7] Antoine Gigal, The Sphinxes of Sheba," Gigal Research, https://www.gigalresearch.com/uk/bulletins-19.php.

[8] Tyson, *She Brought*, 32-3.

Nabonidus); they lived in what is now Iraq (and in the medieval period, a group of Sabians arose in Harran, claiming to be the same sect as that is mentioned in the Quran); they allegedly worshipped the stars (and used astrology), idols (including gold and silver statues of the sun and moon), demons, and fire; ... and they ritually consumed blood.[9]

The Sabians, then, might well have been another sect taking their identity from a cross-section of Nabonidus/Nitocris precedents, i.e., the geographical association with Harran (Nabonidus/Abraham territory); gold and silver statues (cf. Daniel's statues[10]); stars and astrology (Nabonidus' practice); demons (Solomon); fire (Moses); and drinking blood (the Elixir). Might they have called themselves Sabians after the "imbibing" allusion in the "Queen of Sheba" epithet? This would suggest they identified the Queen with the woman of the Song.

The etymology of the Arabic word ṣābi' has been rendered "convert, baptize, etc.," and there is at least one tradition in which Muhammad himself was called a Sabian.[11] Conversion and baptism are forms of initiation, whereby the initiate must study the new way, having rejected the old; this is exactly what Nitocris, in the Song, attempts to do with Nabonidus. She tries to teach him, to convert him; the Elixir is but one of the rites the king is initiated into (but it is the most significant).

It may be the case, therefore, that this "imbibing" perception of Saba/Seba/Sheba, in a ritualistic, cultic context, is attested externally.

---

[9] Haggai Mazuz, "The Identity of the Sabians: Some Insights," in *Jewish Philosophy: Perspectives and Retrospectives*, Dov Schwartz, Raphael Jospe, eds. (Brookline, MA: Academic Studies Press, 2012), 233-54, here 236-51.

[10] Tyson, *Arabian Sinai*, 338-49.

[11] Mazuz, 249.

Riddles

There are no recorded riddles between Solomon and the Queen in the HB, nor between Nabonidus and Nitocris in the Song, nor in the Quran, so what is meant by "she came to test him with hard questions" (1 Kgs 10:1, NRSV)? It would be centuries before anyone even thought to make some up to illustrate the notion. While any alleged example of the secret 'riddles' between two people, in private, many hundreds of years earlier cannot be used as proof of anything in a serious historical analysis, the actual concept of riddles is a fit for the Nabonidus-based interpretations I put forward, as they help to strengthen the argument for a very Babylonian foundation for "Solomon" and a cultic/initiation context for the Queen of Sheba pericope in 1 Kings 10.

Riddles are found in Ancient Egyptian texts and are profoundly popular in Sumerian/Babylonian texts, so much so that they became one of the fundamental tools for training scribes in the *eduba*, the scribal school:

> (What is) a house with a foundation like heaven,
> A house which like a ... vessel has been covered with linen,
> A house which like a goose stands on a (firm) base,
> One with eyes not opened has entered it,
> One with open eyes has come out of it?
> Its solution: the school.
> Tablet from Ur, c. 1750 BCE[12]

It is not surprising that riddles are a staple of the Queen of Sheba legend because Nitocris would have certainly toyed with what was probably one of Nabonidus'

---

[12] Å. W. Sjöberg, "The Old Babylonian Eduba," in *Studies in Honor of Thorkild Jacohsen on his Seventieth Birthday June 7, 1974*, Stephen J. Lieberman, ed., Assyriological Studies 20 (Chicago & London: University of Chicago Press, 1976), 159-79.

favourite pastimes, being a man intent on discovering hidden knowledge.

Nitocris, at Tayma, attempted to keep Nabonidus at bay (sexually) by introducing him to the secret world of her religion, just as the HB claims Solomon was captivated by his wives' foreign deities (1 Kgs 11:4-5). She would have used arcane explanations to extend the learning process, exploiting the king's inherited predilection for riddles and solutions. As the guardian of the Elixir, and of her sacerdotal integrity, she probably *intended* to obscure much from him, so if she kept her part of their deal by giving him riddles, the onus was then upon him to find the answers, rather than her surrendering sacred and forbidden knowledge. In the Song, we can see the learning process over several chapters, with Nabonidus stumbling like a new student, getting things wrong, but finally becoming initiated into several rites.[13]

This is why, I posit, we see in the Queen of Sheba pericope of 1 Kings an echo of the same term, *chidah* ("riddle") from Num 12:8, i.e., the episode in which Miriam and Aaron are overheard gossiping about Moses' "Cushite woman." The subtext to this episode, apart from what I discuss concerning Miriam and Aaron themselves,[14] is that vv. 6-8 represent the formal negation of female-priestly authority. Up to that moment, the priestesses, the seers, the *entu*, etc., held power via their "dark utterances" (riddles) dreams, visions, and omens. They were the ones who served as intermediaries between the deities and the people (kings and priests). Miriam, I have shown, is the historical Ennigaldi-Nanna, Nabonidus' daughter and the first and last *entu* of his reign.

Numbers 12 razes that institution to the ground in a short declaration that these women and their 'mutterings and visions' hold sway no longer, and that the "riddles"

---

[13] For 'initiation' see Tyson, *She Brought*, 120-24.
[14] Tyson, *Arabian Sinai*, 155-60.

are defunct vestiges of a bygone era. For such a refutation of the old ways, the *feminine* old ways, to come in a pericope about the Cushite wife is clearly significant. The castigation in Num 12:6-8 is directed at Ennigaldi (Miriam) and, by extension Nitocris, who was her sacerdotal teacher, previously being a high priestess at Karnak. It is purposefully alluding to the original, perceived power of Nitocris over the king at Tayma; she used her wiles and secret knowledge to seduce him and lead him to ruin. This "art of women" was passed on to her (official) daughter, Ennigaldi. A stereotype was born.

Thus, when 1 Kings describes the visit of the Queen of Sheba, the first thing mentioned is her "testing" of him with "riddles," or "dark utterances," for she was preparing him for his initiation. This is the arcane foundation of the Song of Solomon.

Riddles are also mentioned in Dan 5:12, at the banquet held the night before the fall of Babylon, when Nabonidus supposedly sees a vision on the wall; Daniel is described as one who can solve riddles. The story of Samson and the Philistine woman in Judges 14 has a riddle as a major aspect of the pericope (mentioned eight times), i.e., a riddle coupled with a 'foreign' woman[15] who is accused of, you guessed it, being a prostitute (i.e., "ploughing" is a Mesopotamian sexual euphemism). Riddles were also volleyed between Solomon and Hiram of Tyre, so Josephus tells us (*Ant.* 8.5.3).[16] All three of these riddle stories relate to Nabonidus, as all three characters (Solomon, Samson, and the "king" at the feast,

---

[15] Note that in Gen 21:14, Abraham (Nabonidus) is said to reside "as an alien many days in the land of the Philistines." This might correlate on a historical level, yet to be discerned, with the Samson tales.

[16] Tyson, *Arabian Sinai*, 54-5. I claim this was Hiram III, not Hiram I; Hiram III had been in Babylonia for many years as a royal hostage so the two men must have known each other long before Nabonidus went to Canaan.

aka "Nebuchadnezzar") are his avatars in the HB.[17]

"Seba" is also the figurative *sibling* of Raamah in Genesis 10; Nitocris, in the Song of Solomon, is Nabonidus' *sister*-bride. This may suggest a correlation between Raamah and Nabonidus.

RAAMAH AND NABONIDUS

"Raamah" means "trembling, thundering," from the verb *ra'am*, "to thunder." Thunder in the HB is a theophany of God; in Babylonian lore, too, it pertains to the gods. For instance, Utu the Sun god "thunders over the mountains like a storm" (ETCSL 4.32.2, 27-32), and Inanna "roared like thunder" (ETCSL 1.3.2, 138-43). When Moses speaks with God on Sinai (Exod 19:19), the deity responds in what is interpreted by the crowd as "thunder." I have suggested this is actually a reverberation from calling out against (in front of) the walls that are located on the top of the site in the Hijaz I claim is Sinai.[18] As I suggest this is where Nabonidus and the HB's exodus are to be located in a postexilic world, the etymology of "thunder" in "Raamah" does suggest it is a reference to this region, which implies a connection to Moses/Nabonidus.[19]

If "Raamah" relates to Nabonidus (i.e., at Sinai), then the names of the other siblings, Cush's other "sons," Havilah, Sabtah, and Sabteca, must also correlate somehow with the story of Nabonidus in the HB.

---

[17] See also Ps 49:4, Prov 1:6.

[18] Tyson, *Arabian Sinai*, 218.

[19] It is intriguing that *Hitchcock's Bible Names Dictionary* includes in the definition for "Raamah" the phrase, "some sort of evil." https://biblehub.com/topical/r/raamah.htm.

Havilah

This name suggests "whirling/circling/dance, to drive away, to fall grievously with pain," possibly from the verb *hul* "to be strong" (*hayil* means "might"); or from another *hul*, "to whirl (dance)," or the noun *hil* ("pain"). This would relate to Miriam's musical outburst after crossing the Sea, in Exodus 15; Miriam dies (violently) in Kadesh (Exod 17:1-7; Num 20:1, 9-13).

Havilah is one of the borders of Ishmaelite territory (Gen 25:18), and also the place where Saul fights the Amalekites (1 Sam 15:7). In the exodus narratives, the place where Joshua battles Amalek in Exod 17:8-13, is "Rephidim" (identified with Kadesh, roughly in the same spot a Nabonidus inscription was recently discovered[20]).

Sabtah

Suggests "beating," from *sabat*, "to beat or break." The – *tah* ending may be a play on *ta'*, meaning "chamber," but in Arabic, more an "abode, dwelling" (BDB); or, *ta'a*, "to point out, mark out, boundary."

Sabteca

Also means "beating," from *sabat*, "to beat or break." It may incorporate the verb *ka'a*, "to be disheartened; to be cowed; to be despondent or dejected." In Arabic, this is refined as, "to draw back timidly, abstain through timidity" (BDB).

Both Sabtah and Sabteca have to do with "striking, beating," etc. This is a clear allusion to what happens in

---

[20] Tyson, *Arabian Sinai*, 301-5.

Numbers 20 with the violent attack on Miriam (aka the "rock").[21] Subsequent to this heinous crime, Moses is sent to do battle with Amalek (Exodus 17), to prove himself still worthy of being Israel's leader, but what does he do? He sends Joshua to fight on his behalf and goes and sits on a rock at a distance, with Aaron and Hur holding up his 'tiring' arms. In *Arabian Sinai*, I conjecture that this is Nabonidus trying to get out of facing his awkward past behaviour with the Amalek as drinking buddies. He doesn't want to face them. So the idea of drawing back timidly does seem to resonate; Nabonidus might be getting old by this time but he is an extraordinarily virile man, it would seem. He chooses this action because it suits his nature, i.e., he sends others to do his dirty work (in the slaying of the Midianites, too, amongst other examples).

Sabtah and Sabteca sound similar because they pertain to the same sequence of events in the exodus narratives, and thus the same location. These names are meant to remind us of "Massah and Meribah" (Exod 17:7) which are the two halves of a very special rock that sits just fifty kilometres south of Tayma.[22] A known landmark to the Bedouin for hundreds, if not thousands of years, the rock has recently reached the attention of modern tourists in the area but in Nabonidus' day it served as the last familiar signpost on the arduous journey from the Red Sea to Tayma.

Thus, the "descendants of Cush" are Nitocris and Nabonidus, and the most significant aspects of the exodus story (to the Genesis authors), i.e., the killing of Miriam and the battle with Amalek.

After the mention of Raamah's "sons" (see below) there is an odd interjection into Genesis 10 where we are told that Cush "begat" Nimrod, whose presence on earth

---

[21] Tyson, *Arabian Sinai*, 163-73.
[22] Tyson, *Arabian Sinai*, 161-7.

led to the Mesopotamian nations. The term for begat is *yalad*, "to bear, bring forth, beget"; this is the *only* "son" of Cush presented using begetting terminology, as the others are simply called "descendants" ("sons of" in a generic sense). The name "Nimrod" means "rebel" and is etymologically linked to "Mered," which also means "rebel"; Mered appears in 1 Chronicles 4 as an avatar of Nabonidus.[23] The singling out of Nimrod for this honour of being begotten indicates this is a human, a *real* person, not merely an abstract notion, myth, or allusion. This division of myth and reality is further discussed in my paper on the Genesis 10-11 genealogies.[24]

With "Cush" an allusion to Upper Nubia but also to Nitocris the "Cushite woman," we are expected to make the connection between "Cush" and Babylonia (Nimrod's "Babel"), i.e., the *marriage* between Nitocris and Nabonidus, i.e., the marriage warned against by Daniel (in his allegory of the statue of mixed metals and clay, in Daniel 2),[25] frowned upon by later Jews (Neh 13; 1 Kgs 11), and deemed by the subsequent rabbis to be the harbinger of the fall of Israel (God set in motion the inevitable rise of the Roman Empire on the day the couple consummated their marriage [Avodah Zarah, 1:2, 39c]).

Nimrod, the rebel, is referred to three times in Gen 19:8-9 as being "mighty" (once as a "warrior", twice as a "hunter"). Repetition in quick succession like this is a signal to the readers of the HB to investigate. It is a red flag indicating hidden meaning, almost without exception in my experience. In this case, when we look at the word employed for "mighty," *gibbor*, we learn that in Arabic, the term suggests "one who magnifies himself, behaves

---

[23] Tyson, *She Brought*, 22-4.

[24] Janet Tyson, "Nabonidus and the Arabian Genealogies (Genesis 10 and 11)," www.academia.edu/120828904.

[25] Tyson, *Arabian Sinai*, 339-44; *She Brought*, 140.

proudly, a tyrant, who is bold, audacious"; *gibbor*, stems from the verb *gabar* (rendered "to be strong, mighty"), which in Arabic implies, "compel, force; overbearing behaviour, constraint."

From my perspective as a Nabonidus researcher and a proponent of a wholly exilic-postexilic Torah, it is clear this potential allusion to an Arabic perception of "Nimrod" is intentional and relates directly to Nabonidus himself. He was, indeed, a tyrant, and a proud, conceited man whose "overbearing behaviour" is made all too clear in the Song of Solomon and the tales of the exodus. The "mighty man" epithet also relates to Samson, another avatar of Nabonidus.[26]

We must remember that those of the Israelites who remained with Nabonidus on his return to Tayma would have been strongly influenced by the Arabian milieu; as guests in a foreign land, one of the first things Nabonidus made them do was honour the local custom of the covenant of salt;[27] they were strangers in his old home and peace had to be settled immediately. As scribes influenced, and probably intrigued by the nuances of Arabic as it was in the 6th Century BCE, learning the local language would have added another string to their already impressive literary bows, and another level of meaning not so obviously recognised by all, which is how they worked best.

Thus we see in the very early genealogies, both Nabonidus and Nitocris preserved etymologically on the basis of their most memorable actions: Nabonidus for "beating" the rock, and Nitocris for her blood-Elixir. These two themes are deemed the most important to the authors of Genesis, as they were so significant to the composition of the exodus narratives (written previously).

This is just one of the potential understandings of the

---

[26] Tyson, *She Brought*, 18-20.
[27] Tyson, *Arabian Sinai*, 146-54.

"Queen of Sheba" epithet but it is the most compelling. Nitocris, the "Cushite woman," known for her blood-Elixir which drove Nabonidus to a form of madness, is seen as being responsible for his later irrational behaviour and his eventual fall from grace and exclusion. From the very foundation of the world, it is so claimed, this woman's dark utterances and dark arts were fated to bring the king, and by extension the once idealised Israel, down. And this is just the beginning of the sustained castigation of Nitocris that will persist for centuries, across boundaries of land and faith.

2
Geographical Sheba

IN GEN 10:7, RAAMAH IS SAID TO BE the father of Sheba and Dedan. "Dedan" means "leading slowly," from *dada*, "to move or lead slowly," probably alluding to the iconic camel caravans of the Arabian Desert. Dedan/Dadan, of course, is one of the cities conquered by Nabonidus on his wanderings through Northwest Arabia during his earlier years as King of Babylon.[1]

However, in Gen 25:3, Jokshan is the father of Sheba and Dedan. Does this mean Raamah and Jokshan are identical? I discuss Jokshan later but in this same verse we learn that one of Dedan's "sons" is "Letushim," which means "metalworkers" from *latash*, "to hammer, sharpen." This might refer to the Qenites, i.e., specifically

---

[1] He "walked the road between the cities Tēmā, Dadānu, Padakku, Ḥibrā, Yadīḫu, and (then) as far as Yatribu" (Frauke Weiershäuser and J. Novotny, *The Royal Inscriptions of Amēl-Marduk (561-560 BC), Neriglissar (559-556 BC), and Nabonidus (555-539 BC), Kings of Babylon*, The Royal Inscriptions of the Neo-Babylonian Empire, Vol. 2 [University Park: Eisenbrauns, 2020], Nabonidus 47, i 24-26a).

the itinerant smiths, like Aaron (who I argue lived in this general area).²

The juxtaposition of Sheba with Dedan must be a natural one, a familiar one, but if tradition insists "Sheba" is a location in deepest, southern Arabia, how does this pairing work? There are no Nabonidus inscriptions that can place the Babylonian king in Yemen, but it is far from an impossibility.³ "Dedan" may represent (to the scribes) *all* Arabian nomads, for instance, moving around the sandy landscape in any direction (slowly). It might represent the trade routes that came in and out of Dedan. This difference in perspective, i.e., from the esoteric Elixir of Nitocris' "Seba" to Nabonidus' pragmatic, trade-related "Sheba," is perfectly in tune with the HB's overall depiction of this couple.

This "Sheba," son of Raamah, is possibly linked to the "Saba" mentioned in Tiglath-pileser III's "Inscription 42" (27'b-33') which reads:

> The people of the cities Mas'a (and) **Tema, the (tribe) Saba,** the people of the cities [Ḥayappa, Badanu], (and) Ḫatte, (and) the (tribes) Idiba'ilu, [...], who are on the border of the western lands, [whom none (of my predecessors) had known about, and whose country is remo]te, [heard about] the fame of my majesty (and) [my heroic deeds, and (thus) they beseeched] my lordship. As one, [they brought before me] gold, silver, [camels, she-camels, (and) all types of aromatics] as their payment [and they kissed] my feet.
>
> I appointed [Idibi'ilu as the "gatekeeper" fa]cing Egypt.⁴

---

² Tyson, *Arabian Sinai*, 283, 361-5

³ For instance, there are names in the inscriptions that have yet to be matched with a location.

⁴ Hayim Tadmor and Shigeo Yamada, *The Royal Inscriptions of Tiglath-pileser III, (744-727 BC) and Shalmaneser V (726-722 BC), Kings of Assyria*, The Royal

Tiglath-pileser (744-727 BCE) is boasting about his conquests, i.e., Israel, Gaza, Damascus, etc., and then much farther south, into Northwestern Arabia, defeating Samsi, queen of the Arabs (in this northern region). He mentions Tema alongside a "tribe" called the "Saba." Although they might have been Midianites/Qenites, it would be very interesting if these "Saba" were the HB's Amalek, the wide-ranging, nomadic marauders who would later befriend Nabonidus (I claim) and become an integral aspect of "Moses'" testing at Rephidim (in Exodus 17), which I locate south(south)west of Tayma.[5]

In my previous investigation, I argued that the Amalek were participants in the profane distribution of the Elixir Rubeus; the etymology of their name alludes to a penchant for "licking blood."[6] The verb *saba*, recall, means "to imbibe intoxicating 'wine'" (and "wine" is a known euphemism for blood). The Elixir was known for its ability to induce altered states of consciousness, which is why Nabonidus could become addicted so quickly. In the Song, as mentioned earlier, he invites all and sundry (e.g., the rich and influential from surrounding regions) to partake at Tayma, but goes on to make a business out of it by selling it to wealthy men from a base at the temple in Babylon, noted but not quite understood by Herodotus (*Hist*. 1.199).[7] This is the version of events I gleaned from my analysis of the Song of Solomon, only to find the story continues into the exodus narratives, where the once addicted Nabonidus is tested to prove he has relinquished

---

Inscriptions of the Neo-Assyrian Period Vol. 1 (Winona Lake: Eisenbrauns, 2011), 107 (also, 44.8'b-16'a and 47.Rev.3'-6'a).

[5] It is possible the "Idibi'ilu" were used as the "gatekeeper" on the eastern border of Egypt because they dwelt far enough north for the job; the most important tribe in this area in Nabonidus' time was that of the Qedarites. There is a Saba tribe mentioned in the Quran, e.g., 34.15.

[6] Tyson, *Arabian Sinai*, 174-9.

[7] Tyson, *She Brought*, 207-10.

all association with the Elixir and those with whom he drank, i.e., represented by Amalek.

When the authors of 1 Kings 10 came to write their short account of the Queen of Sheba, I think it is *probable* they knew of the tribe of "Saba," near "Tema," and just like the authors of Exodus, they played with the name for the population surrounding Nabonidus' kingdom, inferring the *notion* of "blood-licking," imbibing allies, and referred to them as "Amalek." The two names would thus be synonymous, reiterate (subliminally) the connection to the Elixir, but be abstract enough not to be inflammatory (some Jews did remain in Tayma). Like using an ancient "Egypt" as the villainous entity that subdued their people, instead of Assyria and Babylon, the scribes were very careful not to risk the ire of those who could still do them harm (e.g., Nabonidus and his followers, and Cambyses).[8]

So, if Raamah's "Sheba and Dedan" are taken as referring to actual locations in Northwestern Arabia, we might suggest Tiglath-pileser's "Mas'a (and) Tema" on the "border of the western lands" corresponds to Dedan and Tayma, as Dedan was also a dynamic trading centre and is often represented in tandem with Tayma (i.e., Hegra became a trading hub for the Nabataeans much later). In Gen 25:14 a descendant of Ishmael is named "Massa," along with "Kedar," "Dumah," and "Tema," etc., all pertaining to Northwestern Arabia (Dedan is conspicuous by its absence).

I have attempted to locate an Assyrian word that might tally with "Mas'a," but the closest I have found is *massû* (fem. "leader") and *massātum* (princess, queen). Might "Mas'a" have been a name signifying that a queen of Arabia ruled there (e.g., the "place of the queens")?[9]

---

[8] Tyson, *Arabian Sinai*, 102-5; 276-7.

[9] The Assyrians sometimes used their own names for

Tiglath-pileser mentions Queen Samsi (in 733 BCE) just before he refers to Mas'a and Tema, so she must have been from this region.[10] If so, perhaps this is why, subsequently, the legend of the "Queen of Sheba" took form so readily; it was a familiar concept that could be exploited.

The point is, "Sheba and Dedan," related to both Raamah (Nabonidus) and Jokshan (Nitocris, see below), are to be taken as two *connected* names, either by proximity or function.

In Gen 16:7, Hagar (Jehudijah), having fled from Abraham (Nabonidus) and Sarah's (Nitocris') home (Tayma), is found by "the spring on the way to Shur." In Exod 18:2 Zipporah (Jehudijah) is returned to Nabonidus by Jethro, while everyone is at Sinai. Sinai, so I explain in *Arabian Sinai*, is the "other Shur" in the exodus narratives, i.e., not the one east of Egypt, which is so obviously avoided, but the one southward, where Moses takes his group (in Northwestern Arabia).[11]

Hagar is discovered by a spring at a place called "Beer-lahai-roi," somewhere between Kadesh and Bered (Gen 16:14). Kadesh, by my reckoning, is the region between Tayma and the Harraat. The etymology of "Bered" suggests a specific location; it stems from the verb *barad*, "to hail." The only place "hail" is significant in the exodus narratives is the Nile Delta, i.e., during the seventh plague of Exodus 9. If we take "Bered" to imply Lower Egypt, then the spring Hagar goes to is somewhere between the Harraat and the Delta, i.e., precisely the territory covered by Nabonidus and his travelling group.

---

conquered places, as explained in Janet Tyson, "Nabonidus, Tarshish, and Ophir" (2024): 14-18, www.academia.edu/120684427.

[10] Tiglath-Pileser III 42 (19'b-22'a); 43 (25'b-21'a). The other Queen of the Arabs mentioned, Zabibe, was farther east, i.e., in northern Syria.

[11] Tyson, *Arabian Sinai,* 129-30.

It is a broad generalisation masked by ambiguity, but it is correct (the authors of Genesis cannot deny the Arabian location but they obscure it so well, it is only today we are beginning to see it again!).

"Beer-lahai-roi" is a composite name, containing allusions to a "well" (*beer*), "living" (*hay*), "to see, seeing" (*ra'a*), and "to write down" (*ba'ar*). Remind you of anywhere? All of these elements pertain to Sinai (i.e., the "living God" whom Moses "sees" face to face, and the writing of the commandments) which, of course, lies between Egypt and Kadesh. However, Sinai is not known for having a well, and whatever springs are extant in the vicinity are probably seasonal and certainly not worth naming for posterity.[12]

Hagar later wanders about in the "wilderness of Beersheba" (Gen 21:14) until the well is revealed to her. The etymology of "Beersheba" suggests a meaning of "well of the oath," or "well of seven," from *be'er*, "well," and either *shaba*, "to swear," or *sheba*, "seven." The name is provided in Gen 21:32, alluding to the agreement made between Abraham and Abimelech, where "seven" lambs are given to Abimelech in exchange for the rights to the well. However, once you realise Genesis is *not* a document that predates Exodus, another option becomes evident, i.e., in Exod 2:15-22 Moses meets Zipporah at the well near her father's home, where she is but one of seven daughters; the two men clearly come to an agreement, and Zipporah given in marriage (in oath). The two wells, of Hagar and of Zipporah, are the same place because the two women are the same person, i.e., Jehudijah.[13]

In my analysis of the exodus narratives, I deduced that the character of Aaron was domiciled somewhere in the Harraat region of northern Arabia, i.e., the volcanic range running along the east coast of the Red Sea; I further

---

[12] Tyson, *Arabian Sinai*, 217.
[13] Tyson, *Arabian Sinai*, 27-30.

deduced that Reuel/Jethro, Moses' father-in-law, was the Qenite leader at Sinai but he did not *live* there. Jethro was Zipporah's father.

Jehudijah, revealed in the Song of Solomon, was already a woman in Nabonidus' harem when Nitocris arrived there in 549 BCE. I suggested she was taken (or given) to the harem from an elite family on the outskirts of Tayma (I hadn't made the connection to Jethro at that time). For her to have been a harem-woman before Nitocris' arrival at Tayma, it seems logical that she was the leader of Tayma's (or at least the high priest's) daughter, taken upon the conquest of the city just a year or two before. Jethro was the "friend" who introduced Nabonidus to the Qenite Yahweh-worship and its metallurgical liturgy.

What I suggest is that the first incident (Genesis 16) depicts a version of what we see happening in the Song of Solomon (6:11-12), i.e., where Nitocris leaves the heart of Tayma and goes into the "valley" in search of a woman whose child she can 'steal' (because she had lied about being pregnant).[14] The valley is where Jehudijah, then pregnant, had been sent for her confinement (I surmised, based on what follows in the Song). So, the spring Hagar first runs to was probably just outside Tayma. Tayma boasts the largest natural well in this part of the world; the Haddaj well, which is fed by over eighty springs; the oasis is praised in Exod 15:27 as the site "Elim," with its seventy palms and twelve springs.[15] Perhaps she thought to make it to Sinai, where Jethro was officiating? Maybe she had balked at Nitocris' initial proposition and tried to flee, to keep her child (and her resentment is palpable in the Song *and* Exodus). The second flight (Genesis 21), to "Beersheba," is therefore the final confirmation that Jehudijah went back *into* Tayma (with her young baby),

---

[14] Tyson, *She Brought*, 157-61.
[15] Tyson, *Arabian Sinai*, 146-7.

under Nitocris' command (i.e., in the Genesis tale, Sarah is told to deal with the matter herself, demonstrating Nabonidus' indifference and/or reticence to get involved in awkward situations).

So, "Beersheba" turns out to be another pseudonym for Tayma,[16] and "Beer-lahai-roi" is the same place, only on the outskirts (probably facing Sinai). Isaac supposedly settled at Beersheba (Gen 25:11); I have argued that Isaac is, on one level, an avatar of Nabonidus' son Belshazzar, who, history seems to suggest, returned to dwell at Tayma.[17]

"Sheba," as a *geographical entity*, therefore, is to be equated with Tayma. With this in mind, the "Queen of Sheba" must then equate with the "Queen of Tayma," who was, of course, Nitocris. The "Sheba and Dedan" that are in the genealogies of both Raamah/Joktan (Nabonidus) and Jokshan (see below), should thus be understood as Tayma and Dedan, the two trading hubs at the centre of Nabonidus' budding commercial empire (before Ophir was integrated). Nitocris can *only* be associated with this period at Tayma (before Ophir) because she died in Babylon at the time of the Persian invasion in 539 BCE (so it seems).[18] It makes sense that she is also seen as the "Queen of the Oath," being the price for peace between Egypt and Babylon (i.e., as a conciliatory bride, in 549 BCE).

It is only when you accept Sheba might be Tayma that another potential understanding of "Queen of Sheba" comes into play: If "Sheba" is Tayma, the name must also *imply* a link to Nabonidus. The name "Sheba," as mentioned earlier, suggests intoxication, e.g., *saba*, a "drunkard." As Nitocris, the guardian of the Elixir, did not partake of the intoxicating potion herself, she cannot be

---

[16] I suggest this is why we see Abraham 'retiring' to "Beersheba" (Gen 22:19).
[17] Tyson, *Arabian Sinai*, 38-40, 139-42.
[18] Tyson, *She Brought*, 225-6.

deemed a "drunkard" but Nabonidus certainly can, given his depiction in the Song of Solomon as the addicted reveller (and in Daniel 5)!

A Strange Coincidence?

In Islam today, there is an aspect of the Hajj (the pilgrimage to Mecca) called the Sa'i. It is a commemoration of Hagar's quest to find water; the legend suggests she went back and forth seven times (i.e., as in the "Well of Seven," or "Beersheba"). The faithful emulate her by traversing the distance between two hills, Safa and Marwah, seven times. The area in which this rite takes place is called "the *mas'a* (the place of hurrying)."[19] Islam would be several hundred years away at the time of Tiglath-pileser, but what an intriguing potential echo of the inscription's "Mas'a." The only conclusion I can draw is that there was a local name for the route between Dedan and Tayma called "Mas'a" (which perhaps Tiglath-pileser picked up on, rather than "Dedan," for some reason, not knowing the area). The rock Moses names "Massah/Meribah" is just about halfway between the two cities.

SHEBA (TAYMA) / SEBA (PUNT)

There are several later uses of both "Sheba" and "Seba" that may help clarify the distinction between these two names, and in doing so, will affirm a potential connection with Punt.

The author of Ps 72:10, for instance, is a Solomon apologist. The psalm begins with a plea for divine

---

[19] Al-Masa'a (Masjid al-Haram), "Madain Project Hajj: Pilgrimage to Mecca," https://www.britishmuseum.org/blog/hajj-pilgrimage-mecca.

protection of the "king" and the "king's son," i.e., this is a standard supplication in Nabonidus inscriptions that plea for Sîn to grant protection for him and Belshazzar, e.g.:

> (As for) me, Nabonidus, the king of Babylon who reveres your great divinity, may I be sated with happiness in life. Moreover, with regard to Belshazzar, (my) first-born son, my own offspring, prolong his days. May he not commit a(ny) sin.[20]

The psalm includes both "Sheba" and "Seba," as places from which kings would bring Solomon gifts; "Tarshish" is also mentioned (in an online paper I argue that Tarshish is Thonis-Heracleion/Naukratis and was the key trading hub for Nabonidus in later years).[21] This might suggest the psalmist is implying that the entire land of eastern Africa, from the Nile Delta to the southern region of Punt were Solomon's suppliers, if not supporters. I think this might well have been the case, especially once Nabonidus had built his successful trading empire on the shores of the Red Sea (with Hiram III of Tyre and Belshazzar). He would, indeed, have had access to produce from this entire region but only because of the political situation of his day, i.e., had "Solomon" lived in the era convention places him in (10th Century BCE), this commercial expansion would not have been possible.[22]

Psalm 72 goes on to include a very interesting request: "May his name endure forever, may his fame

---

[20] Weiershäuser and Novotny, Nabonidus 27, i 32-36.

[21] Tyson, "Nabonidus, Tarshish, and Ophir," 11-13.

[22] In Nabonidus' latter years at Tayma, Persia ruled Egypt and trade was opened up to encourage Arabian (and other) exchange. 10th Century BCE Egypt would not have traded with a miniscule, parochial Jerusalem.

continue as long as the sun" (72:17; and "Blessed be his glorious name forever" in 72:19). Not only does this link the king's name with the "sun," which echoes the hidden text of the exodus narratives,[23] it is in stark contrast to the curse in the Song of Solomon (Song 1:3)[24] that reads something like "Your name is empty/desolation." Then there is "may they pronounce him happy" (72:17), which is an echo of the inscription, above, but also of the (feigned) pregnancy pericope of Song (6:9), i.e., a subtle link to Leah's proclamation of pregnancy (Gen 30:13) suggests an allusion to Nitocris and her pregnancy.[25]

The author has taken what the Song and the exodus narratives have preserved concerning Nabonidus and have turned it all on its head (especially with the gushing praise about his charitable and empathetic nature, which the said texts *utterly* refute). He has used familiar names (which hold power) to reverse the curses and the negative judgements.

When Ezek 27:22 suggests that "the merchants of Sheba and Raamah," were Tyre's merchants, trading spices, gems, and gold, this is potentially a reference to "Raamah" as Nabonidus, and "Sheba" as Tayma. Nabonidus certainly was a key figure in Hiram of Tyre's trading expeditions, and much of what we see them dealing with is gold and fine products that would have come from "Ophir," i.e., Punt.

Sheba is listed again in the next verse, as trading fine "clothes of blue" and colourful carpets. When you check what kinds of clothing were worn in ancient Arabia (as far as can be surmised), it is very obvious that styles, and even

---

[23] In Ps 72:5, his lifespan is compared to that of the sun and the moon, but in v. 7, the implication of "until the moon is no more" is that peace will "flourish" all the days of his life, for he *is* "the moon" in both the exodus narratives and the Song.

[24] Tyson, *She Brought*, 49-50.

[25] Tyson, *She Brought*, 153.

colours, were very regional. In the coastal Hijaz, for instance, the Bedouin wore "locally-dyed indigo cloth ... with ... colourful embroidery and other embellishments," while in the south, colours were muted, often dark, highlighted perhaps by a colourful belt. From the Hijaz region a particular embroidery stitch was apparently transferred, via trade, into Western embroidery, allegedly via Spain,[26] i.e., trade which would have been conducted either through Tyre or Thonis.

"Of what use to me is frankincense from Sheba or sweet cane from a distant land?" (Jer 6:20); if Sheba were the Yemen, wouldn't this also be considered a "distant land" to someone living in Jerusalem? The Frankincense Trail passed right through Tayma; it is far more likely someone in Jerusalem would know of Tayma, the centre of the exiles' existence for so many years, than some "distant" city much farther south (and note how the source of the "cane" is not named, i.e., probably not known). [27]

On the other hand, in Isa 43:3 (cf. 45:14), a list of three nations is provided, i.e., Yahweh is claiming he has used these places as "ransom" for Israel: Egypt, Nubia (Ethiopia), and Seba. This suggests Seba is south of Egypt, and south of Nubia (most lists in the HB run from eldest to youngest for people, and in a chosen trajectory for locations). The geographical Seba, then, seems to be Punt, in or near modern-day Eritrea. Mill's discussion on Strabo's "Saba" is interesting and also suggests this location relates to "Saba, son of Cush."[28] The location of

---

[26] Heather Colyer Ross, "The Fabric of Tradition," *Saudi Aramco World* (Sept/Oct, 1987): 21-9.

[27] Recall that in the quotation from Tiglath-pileser, above, those coming from Mas'a and Tema, and the other towns in the "western lands," bring him incense/spices ("aromatics") as their "payment."

[28] Donald K. Mills, "Thutmose III, Hatshepsut, Emmet Sweeney, and the Location of Punt," Part 3, *Chronology and*

Geographical Sheba

Strabo's Saba[29] is only slightly north of where I suggest Ophir/Punt is (in *Arabian Sinai*) and is in the general location of where many now consider Punt to be.[30]

The ancient Egyptians referred to their land as "Blackland" and "Redland," the former being the Nile region, with its fertile soil, the latter the desert on either side of Egypt. *Graffito* left by Sankhkare Mentuhotep III (2009-1997 BCE), at He(ne)nu in the Wadi Hammamat, refers to Punt as being in the "Redland":

> [My lord – ... [has] sent [me] to lead the vessels to Punt in order to bring for him the fresh myrrh from the possession of the rulers, having the authority over the Redland thanks to the fear of him throughout the foreign lands.[31]

In the preamble of Hatshepsut's account of the expedition, an oracle states:

> I have led them on water and on land, to explore the waters of inaccessible channels, and I have reached the Myrrh-terraces.[32]

The expedition clearly had to travel inland from the Red Sea via river tributaries to reach the interior myrrh terraces. Punt's designation as part of the "Redland" under

---

Catastrophism Review 1 (2022): 22, https://www.academia.edu/79188472.

[29] Mills, "Part 3," 22.

[30] Tyson, "Nabonidus, Tarshish, and Ophir," 35-42.

[31] Filip Taterka, "Hatshepsut's Expedition to the Land of Punt: Novelty or Tradition?," *Current Research in Egyptology 2015: Proceedings of the Sixteenth Annual Symposium University of Oxford, United Kingdom 15-18 April 2015*, Christelle Alvarez, et al. eds. (Oxbow Books, 2016), 114-23, here 118.

[32] J. H. Breasted, *Ancient Records of Egypt* (New York, 1962), 5 Vols., 116, #288.

the "authority" of Amun-Re, means it *had* to have been within the same stretch of desert that ran, roughly, from the eastern Nile Delta, all the way to the far end of Nubia. Suggesting Punt lay anywhere else, e.g., western, or even southern Africa, Canaan, or Arabia, just doesn't make sense.

So, the geographical "Sheba" is identified with Tayma, and "Seba" with Punt.

When you think about it, it is fitting for Genesis' "Seba" (Punt) to be a) the 'descendant' of "Cush" (Nubia) and b) the 'ancestor' of "Sheba" (Tayma):

a) Punt is the 'offspring' of Nubia: the trading site would have come later than the nation itself.

b) Punt was a far more ancient trading site than Tayma, having been a source of trade for Egypt from the 4th Dynasty (2613 to 2494 BCE).

When Joktan's "descendants" (i.e., I suggest this is another avatar of Nabonidus; see the next chapter) are listed (Gen 10:26-9), "Sheba" is there, but "Dedan" is not; "Ophir" is there, instead. To me, this suggests "Raamah" represents Nabonidus in his first phase at Tayma, i.e., when the importance of Dedan as a trading hub was more important (than in later years), and when the link to "imbibing" was even more significant ("Sheba" being the first of the two names mentioned, giving it superiority). In the second phase of his stay, as Joktan (post-539 BCE), Sheba retains a position in the list but is bumped down to tenth in line (i.e., we know from the exodus narratives that Nabonidus retained his association with the Elixir but that there was a concerted effort to rid him of his habit). Ophir takes Dedan's place in the commercial sphere; as "Solomon" at Tayma, Nabonidus is the one with ships at Ezion-geber that travel to Ophir for gold, etc. In a paper online, I explain this further, i.e., that "Ophir" is another name for Punt, used solely in connection with Nabonidus (and it has another more sinister understanding), and that "Ezion-geber" was Nabonidus' port on the Red Sea; we now call it al-Wajh.[33]

---

[33] Tyson, "Tarshish, and Ophir"; *Arabian Sinai*, 130-6. Every one of the names of Joktan's descendants is also an encapsulated allusion to a place, person, or event we find in the exodus narratives.

3

Keturah

THE LINK BETWEEN ABRAHAM'S final partner Keturah and the Queen of Sheba is very subtle but I think it is necessary to include this character, as 'she' links together several themes and events that might help us to understand the context in which the later "Queen of Sheba" legends arose, specifically in Arabia.

Certain sages proposed that "Keturah" and "Hagar" are identical characters (Gen. Rabbah 61:4), which I find intriguing, though in this instance, consider erroneous. Others have argued that Abraham must have married three times, and that Keturah was his third spouse, based on Gen 25:1: "Abraham took another wife/woman." Then there is the debate about Keturah being a true wife or a concubine, based on the statement in 1 Chr 1:32 that she was the "concubine of Abraham"; some even suggest Hagar, once a concubine, was finally married to Abraham.[1] This latter

---

[1] For concise discussions of the traditional arguments see Tamar Kadari, "Keturah: Midrash and Aggadah" (20 March

suggestion may have *some* substance but it is tenuous, as the exodus narratives include a pericope involving Jehudijah (whose avatar in Genesis is "Hagar") in which Nabonidus is alluded to as a "husband" but the scene is far from straightforward and involves Jehudijah's daughter, so my guess, given what I have discovered about Jehudijah, is that she would *not* have married Nabonidus after everything he had put her through.

However, *before* the Sinai years, Jehudijah had been the king's ("Solomon's") concubine at Tayma. The Song of Solomon, written by this woman, conveys the passion of an unrequited love for Nabonidus; she is the voice behind every verse of the Song's longing, despair, joy, etc., even though the leading woman in the action of the narrative is Nitocris. That is why there seems to be three people in the Song, when the narrative itself contains only two. Jehudijah was enamoured with the king from afar; when it was her turn to be visited by the king (sexually), she got pregnant and was moved to the "valley" to give birth. Nitocris found her, made a deal to secure the female child as her own, and kept Jehudijah on as wet nurse.

When Nabonidus, blind to all Nitocris' ploys and ruses, failed to acknowledge Jehudijah, the scales fell from her eyes and she began the tale of the Song, probably during her few years at the temple at Ur. By the time the exodus was underway, the Song was already in circulation and Jehudijah had amassed a following of her own. As trouble upon trouble seemed to reveal Nabonidus' true nature, Jehudijah, who had been forced to join the exodus,[2]

2009), The Shalvi/Hyman Encyclopedia of Jewish Women, Jewish Women's Archive, https://jwa.org; Levi Avtzon, "Who Was Keturah and Why Did Abraham Marry Her?," www.chabad.org; Emil G. Hirsch, M. Seligsohn, Jewish Encyclopedia, "Keturah," https://www.jewish encyclopedia .com; Eric Lyons, "Was Keturah Abraham's Wife or Concubine?" (December 31, 2002), https://apologeticspress .org.

[2] Tyson, *Arabian Sinai*, 64-7.

grew ever more resentful, becoming a thorn in Nabonidus' side with her accusations against him.

I claim in *Arabian Sinai* that Jehudijah is Nabonidus' second-wife, to distinguish her from Nitocris, the true wife (deceased). At court she was a concubine that bore him a child, so her status would have been raised by that event. She sat midway, so to speak, in the hierarchy of the king's women. It is because Keturah is described in ambiguous terms, i.e., in Gen 25:1 as the *ishah* of Abraham ("wife/woman"), and in 1 Chr 1:32 as his *pilegesh* ("concubine"), some interpreters suggest she must be Hagar, but this is not supported by the extant texts.

Nabonidus was blissfully unaware of Nitocris' deception until well into the exodus years, by which time Jehudijah and he had very little to say to each other. Jehudijah was killed on the outskirts of Sinai, on Nabonidus' orders, so she could not have borne him six more children.[3]

So no, I cannot agree that Keturah is meant to be Hagar.

As for the etymology of "Keturah," there are debates about that, too. The most common translation is "incense," from *qatar*, "to produce smoke." In Deut 33:10, *qetorah* is used to mean "incense"; in Gen 19:28, the "thick smoke" (*qitor*) is from the destruction of Sodom and Gomorrah, which I suggest is part of the volcanic Haraat (Arabia); in Exod 30:1 there is *miqtar*, a "place of sacrificial smoke" needed to burn the incense, i.e., the *qetoreth*.

In the Song of Solomon, one of the most easily visualised scenes is that of the king's caravan coming up from the desert toward Tayma amidst the perfumed smoke (Song 3:6). This is set in a context of the arrival of the royal couple at Tayma from Egypt, following the incense

---

[3] Tyson, *Arabian Sinai*, 352-8.

trade route through Tayma, i.e., the camels loaded with frankincense, myrrh, and spices.[4]

An alternative insight is based on the argument that "Keturah" is an Aramaic name and therefore indicates that the character hailed from eastern Syria, and that the etymology is from *qṭwr* "strongly bound"; the noun *qṭwr*, can mean "a blow," and this is understood to suggest the notion of a hammer striking a nail to "forcibly" bind two things together.[5]

This is a *possible* etymology but I would not go with this explanation of why it might be used. As there are alternative translations for words of the same spelling in Aramaic as in Hebrew, I think there is a better suggestion for this "bound" idea. The Comprehensive Aramaic Lexicon lists other options for *qṭwr*: "smoke," "blow," "amulet," and "one who binds with a spell."[6]

My very first impression of Keturah was that she was another avatar of Nitocris, added by a later author who wasn't content with the treatment of her (as Sarah) in the exodus narratives, and so added this Arabian genealogy to finally put to rest any possible misunderstanding about her relationship with "Isaac." The veritable expulsion of Keturah's offspring into Arabia is a parallel to Ishmael's (and that is why they are mentioned together in Gen 25:1-18); effectively, it leaves Nitocris 'out there', stranded in the desert (like the scapegoat she became) away from Israel, along with all the other Arabian non-Jews associated with Nabonidus.

The emphasis on incense was also leading me to

---

[4] Tyson, *She Brought*, 83-4.

[5] Jim Stinehart, "Aramaic Names in Genesis," 3. Keturah (March 18, 2016), and "Keturah: The Back Story," (March 19, 2016), B-Hebrew: The Biblical Hebrew Forum, http://bhebrew.biblicalhumanities.org.

[6] Comprehensive Aramaic Lexicon Project, "*qṭwr*," https://cal.huc.edu.

Nitocris who, in the Song, is constantly enveloped in exotic fragrances, spices, and oils. Solomon's daughters, Taphath and Basemath, are also given incense-related names in 1 Kgs 4:11, 13. "Taphath" is derived from the verb *nataph*, which suggests dripping; the same word is employed in Song 4:11; 5:5, 13, in reference to the dripping of honey and "liquid myrrh." "Basemath," from *bosem*, means "fragrance," i.e., a spicy, sweet odour. Both daughters reflect the fundamental character/nature of Nitocris of the Song, in that they are identified with the "liquid myrrh" and spices of the Elixir Rubeus.[7]

So, if Keturah is another representation of Nabonidus' wife, Nitocris, the other suggestions for *qtwr* make far more sense than hitting something with a hammer, for in Song 8:6, Nitocris (through the voice of Jehudijah, the author), calls on the king to "set [her] as a seal upon [his] arm." She alludes to a metaphorical amulet worn as a sign of an oath, i.e., an oath that binds the king to her in a far more profound way than a "blow." Also, throughout the Song, and in later rabbinical texts, Nitocris is depicted as a scheming sorceress, casting her heinous spells on the king. These two alternative understandings relate most suitably to "Keturah," perhaps.

It should also be noted that "Keturah" might be a play on *ketubbah*, for this is the Hebrew term for a marriage contract. In contrast, when you look at the language of Exod 2:21, where "Zipporah" (who is also Jehudijah) is given to Moses, the NRSV says Reuel gave Moses his daughter "in marriage," but the Hebrew text actually says Reuel gave his daughter "to live with" Moses, using the verb *yashab*, "to sit, remain, dwell." That's quite a difference. I have claimed this scene with Zipporah corresponds to the acquisition of Jehudijah as a woman of the harem at Tayma, i.e., as a concubine.[8] So,

---

[7] Tyson, *She Brought*, 23.
[8] Tyson, *Arabian Sinai*, 27-30.

the potential, ironic play on *ketubbah* might be in order to subjugate "Keturah" by suggesting the "marriage" was not legitimate (and this theme is significant in Daniel 2's warning of the weakened statue, and even in the Gospel of John's allegory of the "husbands" that were not "husbands" of the Samaritan woman [Jn 4:16-18]).

This rejection of Nitocris, via a superficially positive name, that hides within it a few sinister reminders of the woman the early Jews loved to hate, suits a predominantly anti-Nitocris HB, and is just one of many such applications of subliminal etymology used to suppress the significance of powerful women in the HB.

KETURAH AS METAPHOR

If you had to encapsulate "Arabia" in one word, what would you choose? "Sand"? "Heat"? Not very romantic, perhaps; not very symbolic. "Incense," on the other hand, is so evocative; it lends itself to daydreams, memories, sacredness, and intoxicating stimuli. It *is* one of the most iconic perceptions of exotic Arabia, especially in an era of new discoveries, growing trade routes, and increasing opulence.

As I have explained in *Arabian Sinai*, Nitocris had died almost as soon as Cyrus entered Babylon, and so the avatar "Sarah" became part of a necessary scribal technique to incorporate the significance of Nitocris in the early Jewish history. She was never in Canaan. After her death, in real life, Nabonidus left Babylon with a handful of Israelites and travelled through Canaan (as "Abraham") with, effectively, the ghost of his wife tagging along. It was always Nabonidus' desire to return to Tayma, I have argued; he had become an honorary Arab. He went native. After the Sinai years, so I suggest, the ex-king returned to his beloved Tayma, serving as a local king-figure-cum-high-priest and building his trading empire (with Belshazzar).

It is a common enough adage that a man can be married to his work, or a car becomes the other "she" in a marriage, etc., so here, I put it that Nabonidus' (Abraham's) most enigmatic and Arabian-nuanced partner, the "other woman" after Sarah's demise, is none other than the love of his life, Arabia.

The "concubine" stereotype in the HB, the *pilegesh*, is obviously known for one thing: Sex. It is not a term of endearment, nor is there really any politically-correct version of it in this period. It strongly relates to the Babylonian depiction of the goddess Ishtar (Marduk's concubine/consort) as the sexually-liberated *zonah*, or "harlot." The exilic Jews' rejection of Ishtar's influence on their lives shaped their subsequent perception of women, and even became a strong element in the tale of Moses turning the Nile to blood.[9]

> ... the *pilegesh* was associated with sexual behavior .... [The term] *pilegesh* is used in the Bible as part of a literary motif rather than as an indication of a particular status, and that there is no necessary association of the *pilegesh* with slavery. The *pilegesh* is outside the family; his or her sexuality is not licit in the normative sense and leads to disinheritance or death. It is the *pilegesh*, not the slave, who is the true "other."[10]

---

[9] Tyson, *Arabian Sinai*, 105-7.

[10] Diane Kriger, *Sex Rewarded, Sex Punished: A Study of the Status of "Female Slave" in Early Jewish Law* (Boston: Academic Studies Press, 2011), 91.

Genesis' "wife" title was conferred on Keturah because she was associated with the man the authors honoured, i.e., the Nabonidus *they* knew as the one who took them home, to Canaan. Genesis, despite the hidden etymological allusions to his faults and ultimate censure (which is in keeping with a 'divine dictate' to write everything down, truthfully), is a fairly pro-Nabonidus text, along with most of Deuteronomy, at least compared to the anti-Nabonidus Exodus and Numbers, so I don't find it in the least surprising that his partner in latter years would be presented in polite terms. Genesis deals with the genealogical implications, the unsavoury bits of the "truth," by telling the story of Hagar and Ishmael, and in the clever etymology of Keturah's children. They skirt around the issues very carefully.

By the time of 1 Chronicles, however, any previous sense of obligation or gratitude toward Nabonidus had been degraded by years of Jewish self-assessment and rationalisation. The post-Sinai period, I have claimed, is when the elderly Nabonidus really came into his own as an international tycoon. He *became* the "King Solomon" we find in Kings and Chronicles (though the nature of "Solomon" is forged in the Song of Solomon, long predating the latter two texts). His wealth, his insatiable proclivities, e.g., for gold, silver, horses, women, etc., are a gaudy demonstration of decades of wheeling and dealing, of 'special handshakes' with old buddies (also ex-kings), and a relentless drive to have more of everything. Resentment of him grew as his audacity and extravagance increased, while the Jews recently returned from exile were still struggling in Jerusalem. He became a stereotype of himself, a caricature, almost; he became the dreaded "666" (more on this later).[11]

For the early Jews, in time, the link to Arabia grated and had to be dealt with more directly. Addenda were

---

[11] Tyson, *Arabian Sinai*, 346-9.

added to the early accounts of the exodus, for instance, and toponyms commandeered, to help the transition from a predominantly Arabian phenomenon to one that sat neatly within the boundaries of Jewish territory. Genesis was written, I argue, long after the exodus years, in an effort to place everyone in their right places, so that the Jewish identity might move forward, well and truly rooted in the Canaan they had so recently conquered with the help of the Babylonian military general, Belshazzar (as "Joshua").

Thus we see "Keturah" presented in a later 1 Chronicles as this sexualised "other," an illicit, exploited entity, i.e., she becomes Arabia the nemesis, Arabia the lusted after, the *pilegesh* to be exploited for its treasures whilst keeping it at a distance and disavowed.

Several of the *pilagshim* in the HB are "associated with sexual assaults" (e.g., Gen 35:22; Judg 19-21; 2 Sam 3:7); this appears to serve a "literary function," in that they attract danger, which leads to chaos."[12] In an ancient "Arabia v. Jerusalem" context, it is not hard to see how this simple shift in depicting "Keturah" might have been the tip of the iceberg, especially when you read Ezekiel 23's diatribe against Samaria and Jerusalem, i.e., in terms of marriage, adultery, and *pilagshim*. The beloved "wife" and the damned "concubine/ harlot" are two sides of the same metaphor, only involving entire nations, rather than individuals.

Arabia ("Keturah") became the intoxicating, all-consuming substitute for Nitocris (Sarah) and the Elixir. In a way, perhaps, you could say that Keturah and the Queen of Sheba are mirror-images of each other, in that they represent the same basic thing, i.e., Nabonidus' illicit addictions.

---

[12] Kriger, 90; 101.

Arabian Progeny

In Genesis 25 we learn the names of Abraham's sons with Keturah, that is, Nabonidus' legacy in Arabia (cf. Josephus, *Ant.* 1.15):

Zimran

This means something like "making music" but can also suggest "pruning"; from *zamar,* "to sing or praise" or "to prune." There are two nouns both spelt *zamir*; one means "a trimming or pruning" but the other means "psalmist, singing, song." Song 2:12 is one of seven HB uses of this word, i.e., "the time of singing has come." The noun *zimra* also means "song." "Zimran" is etymologically linked to "Zimri," the name of the character stabbed through with a spear by Phinehas (Num 25:6-16).

I postulate in *Arabian Sinai* that Zimri may well be another avatar of Aaron; Aaron's death is highly suspicious and I attempt to demonstrate in that discussion that it seems possible both he and Jehudijah were killed together (Aaron was a goldsmith, and one of the traditional side-lines of this very ritualistic and sacerdotal office was to be a musician. Jehudijah was a songstress/poet, who would have been accompanied by a musician during recitals[13]). I therefore suggest that etymological continuity points to Zimran also being linked to Aaron in this alternative context.

I would stick to the "singing/song" understanding, myself, but if pushed to include the concept of "cutting/pruning," I would interpret this metaphorically, i.e., Aaron/Zimri is 'cut down' by a sharp implement.

---

[13] Tyson, *Arabian Sinai*, 353-8; 360-1.

Jokshan

See below.

Medan

Means "strife," or "contention/conflict"; *madon* means "strife, discord."

Midian

Means "strife," or "contention/conflict"; *madon* means "strife, discord."

Again, we see the pairing of two almost identical names that bring to mind the naming of the rock at Rephidim/Kadesh ("Massah and Meribah"), where Moses strikes the rock and where he has to contend with Amalek (Numbers 20 and Exodus 17). This seems to be one of the most striking (pun intended) memories of the exodus years, as it is alluded to often and with due cause, for it was the defining moment for "Moses" and the ultimate proof for the Israelites on the (extended) exodus that Nabonidus was not the man they wished to emulate or retain in any position of authority in their new land.

Ishbak

Means "one who leaves, quits, etc." from *shabaq*, "to leave, forsake, quit." Ishmael leaves and settles in Arabia, i.e., another defining moment so often underappreciated, as it represents the overriding rejection of Nabonidus' "people" from the community of the Israelites who crossed over into Canaan.

Shuah

Suggests "to sink down, melt, subside," or "depression, excavation, reservoir," from *shuah*, with the same meanings.

This, to me, is most certainly an allusion to the "manna" that is said to "melt" or disappear, etc.; the manna which I claim was natural salt, gathered at Tayma's sabkha.[14] A sabkha is a depression that was once a lake ("reservoir"), that has dried out but when replenished by heavy dew or subsurface water, creates the perfect environment for a surface crust of salt. Heated by the sun, the manna "melts" (*masas*), according to Exod 16:21: The sabkha goes through a cyclical process, i.e., moisture enters the system (often overnight) then it continually evaporates, leaving salt crystals on the surface; when these get heavy enough, they slowly sink below the crust.[15] To those unfamiliar with the scientific process, it would, indeed, seem as though the crystals were dissolving or melting.

Abarim Publications offers a potential understanding of "salvation" from *shawa*, "to cry out (for salvation)," or *yasha'*, "to save." Strong's suggests "avenging, defend, deliverer, help, preserve, rescue, be safe." And several Bible dictionaries offer "wealth, prosperity," from *shoa'*, meaning "financially independent," or "rich."

These two concepts of "salvation" and "wealth" link to the new perception of Belshazzar I provide in *Arabian Sinai*, i.e., he has several avatars in the HB but the most significant is "Joshua," whose name means "Yah saves, Yah is salvation" (from *yah*, "God," and the verb *yasha'*, "to save") but whose original name, "Hoshea" meant, simply, "salvation." He was once crown prince of

---

[14] Tyson, *Arabian Sinai*, 148-54.
[15] Mohammad and Awadh, 268-9.

Babylon, effectively a regent to an absent Nabonidus, but from I can discern from the exodus narratives, he subsequently became his father's business partner in Tayma. He is linked to at least one instance, both in the HB *and externally*, in which "wealth" plays a central role.[16] He was the son of one of the richest men in the world at the time. There are scholars (including me) who argue that Belshazzar returned to Tayma after the fall of Babylon.[17]

JOK-SHAN

I first considered "Jokshan" to be a representation of Nitocris, as the name means "one who ensnares," from *yaqosh* or *qush*, "to lay a snare," or "to lure, entrap, etc." Going right back to the Song of Solomon, Nitocris is depicted as a relentless huntress, forever setting a trap for the king, using her feminine wiles to seduce him, to trick him, to keep him from his duties and to turn his devotions to her gods. The allusions to "snares/snaring" in the Song are plentiful and this is just the sort of subliminal wordplay the HB authors frequently employ in their incessant denigration of the Egyptian princess. Note also, that *qush* is a play on Cush/Kush in the epithet of "the Cushite woman" given to Nitocris in the exodus narratives.

This convinced me until I began to find discrepancies; it was a case of "practise what you preach" for me, as I always claim that I never force an interpretation, yet I came across data that just didn't fit, so I had to rethink this one. It may yet need more work, but let's look at the rest of the analysis and you can decide

---

[16] Tyson, *Arabian Sinai*, 139-42.

[17] Paul-Alain Beaulieu, *The Reign of Nabonidus King of Babylon 556-539 B.C.* (New Haven: Yale, University Press, 1989), 203-5. Tyson, *Arabian Sinai*, 36-40.

which character this name fits best.

If we take the two components to be "Jok" (*Yok/Yoq*) and "shan," what might this tell us?

★ "Jokim" (*Yoqim*) is mentioned as a son of Shelah of Judah (1 Chr 4:22), but the first Shelah is a descendant (son) of Arpachshad (Gen 11:14), who is an abstract rendition of Nabonidus.[18] The noun *qim* denotes an adversary or enemy; if "Jo" (*Yo*) is taken to refer to God (*Yah*), this may suggest "enemy of God" (which is how Nabonidus is later perceived by the Jews). There is also a "Jakim" in 1 Chr 24:12, a descendant of Eleazar and Ithamar, the 'sons' of Aaron. This identification, given the context of the Arabian exodus, would again suggest a near-Tayma location, for Aaron and Ithamar both dwell in the Harraat region (according to my investigations).

★ Then there is Jochebed (*Yokheved/Yokebed*), who, in Exod 6:20 is named as the mother of Moses and Aaron. I discuss this character in her symbolic role as "mother," in *Arabian Sinai*.[19]

★ In 2 Kgs 14:7 there is "Joktheel" (*Yoqtheel*) which is a toponym, supposedly created by King Amaziah after his conquest of Sela, i.e., the same Sela where Nabonidus he left a large rock inscription.[20] The name first appears in the HB, however, in Josh 15:38 as a territory allotted to Judah.

---

[18] "Nabonidus and the Arabian Genealogies (Genesis 10 and 11)," www.academia.edu/120828904.

[19] Tyson, *Arabian Sinai*, 245-50.

[20] Frauke Weiershäuser and J. Novotny, *The Royal Inscriptions of Amēl-Marduk (561-560 BC), Neriglissar (559-556 BC), and Nabonidus (555-539 BC), Kings of Babylon*, The Royal Inscriptions of the Neo-Babylonian Empire, Vol. 2 (University Park: Eisenbrauns, 2020), Nabonidus 55.

✯ There is a certain "Jekuthiel" (*Yequthiel*), son of Mered (Nabonidus) and Jehudijah (1 Chr 4:18).

✯ Most significantly, there is "Joktan," representing Nabonidus.[21] The name means something like "he will be made little," from *qaton*, "to be small." In *She Brought*, I claim there are two curses in the Song, one against Nabonidus ("Solomon") and the other against Nitocris (his Egyptian wife). For Solomon, the author encodes a phrase akin to: "his name is worthless." This is why we cannot read Nabonidus' name anywhere in the Bible; it was considered anathema by the early HB authors. "Joktan" thus becomes one of many slurs against the ex-king, anticipating several biblical texts and their attempt to bring low, humiliate, and otherwise "make little" the once arrogant and very much disliked Nabonidus (e.g., Exodus, Numbers, Song of Solomon, Daniel). More amazingly, perhaps, in the Arabic tradition, "Joktan" can also mean "to strike or beat"; this is what Moses is known for, i.e., in Exodus he strikes an Egyptian, the Nile, etc., but in Numbers, he strikes the "rock" ("Miriam") and it is for this act he is denied the right to enter Canaan. This is the basis for the repeated Massah/Meribah allusions.

There are a few others, including some very interesting related names, such as Jakeh, from Proverbs 30. There is much debate and confusion about whether or not Prov 30:1 contains three names, i.e., Agur, Ithiel, and Ucal,[22] or if these words are simply "compiler," "weary," and "prevail." The *Jewish Encyclopedia*, however, claims that the text of 30:1 seems to say that he (Agur) was a

---

[21] Tyson, "Arabian Genealogies," www.academia.edu/120828904.

[22] I am intrigued by the repetition here, i.e., two Ithiels and then one Ucal. Is this code? This is similar to the pattern I discerned in the Song of Solomon, entailing a 2-3 pattern for the name of "Solomon," which turned out to be the secret 'signature' of the author, Jehudijah (see *She Brought*, 216-17).

'Massaite'";[23] that is, he is from the same geographic area as Genesis 25's "Massa." If the latter can be related to Tiglath-pileser's "Mas'a," near Tayma (Tema), this would certainly suggest Proverb 30 was written with "Solomon" in mind, i.e., with Nabonidus in mind. Just as Ecclesiastes is alleged to be Solomon's retrospective thoughts (very reminiscent of the Song of Solomon, and reads like someone imagined what the king of the Song would think of his own life and dubious choices), though clearly composed much later by an anonymous author. Proverbs 30 is a precursor, perhaps, i.e., one of the first attempts to rationalise Nabonidus' involvement with the early Jews (by doing some damage limitation). Note how the last line of Proverbs 30 is "pressing anger produces strife"; here we have yet another allusion to the *context* of "Massah and Meribah" that seems to be highlighting Moses' angry outburst at Rephidim-Kadesh (the "place of strife"), but also to the name "Massah."[24]

The overall impression is that names of this type are somehow linked to Nabonidus.[25]

And what of the second element of Jokshan, "shan"?

★ The first potential connection I found was the verb *shaan*, which means "to lean, support oneself." This relates to Song 8:5, which speaks of the arrival of Nitocris and the young Ennigaldi-Nanna at Ur, having

---

[23] J. Frederic McCurdy, Louis Ginzberg, "Agur ben Jakeh," *Jewish Encyclopedia*, https://www.jewishencyclopedia.com.

[24] Recall the discussion concerning the Islamic "Mas'a," and the potentially symbolic route between Tayma and Dedan (pg. 25).

[25] The modern Jewish word "Yok" suggests a non-Jew, a gentile, etc., and is pejorative. It is thought to stem from a reversal of *goy* ("people") but I wonder if its roots are a lot older.

left Tayma in 543 BCE.[26] Nitocris leans against the king in a feigned display of feminine weakness.

* The noun *shen* means "tooth," from the verb *shanan*, "to sharpen," or "to teach diligently, to inculcate," relating to Nitocris' allegedly idolatrous ways and tutelage (of Nabonidus). This alludes to Song 4:2.[27]
* The verb *sane'* means "to reject"; the adjective *sani'* suggests something that is "hated."
* The element "shan" sits in the middle of the word *shushan, shoshan, shoshannah*. This is the "lily" of the Song of Solomon.
* The term *shani* means "red, scarlet"; this pertains to Song 4:3 and the "crimson cord" of the woman's "lips"; this is a highly symbolic turn of phrase in the Song pointing directly to the Elixir Rubeus rite (and to Ishtar).[28]

The "shan" element is very strongly Nitocris-based, except for the fact that in the Song of Solomon, the author, Jehudijah, tells her tale on two levels: Nitocris is the central female character who performs all the actions attributed to her, but the inner thoughts, the mood, and the emotions are predominantly Jehudijah's. It is *her* voice we hear at the heart of the narrative. Nitocris is *not* the "lily of the valley"—Jehudijah is (i.e., the "lily" the king impregnates, who dwells in the "valley" during her confinement).

So, "Jokshan" is, for my money, a definite example of a woman being purposefully hidden amongst the men. I also think that the etymology of her name is purposefully

---

[26] Tyson, *She Brought*, 193-4.
[27] Tyson, *She Brought*, 95.
[28] Tyson, *She Brought*, 95-7.

ambiguous in an effort to allude to the Song itself, which would be remarkably clever but so apt. As the name appears in the list of Keturah's descendants, who are all destined to reside in Arabia, and as Nitocris already has her place in the "Cush" list, I do wonder whether "Jokshan" is more suitably Jehudijah, or if we must retain a dual identification, just as in the Song. One might even suggest that the main "ensnaring" definition of "Jokshan" is applied to women in general, which would also be apropos (recalling the *yeser*, etc.).

There are other factors to consider. For instance, "Sheba and Dedan" are deemed the sons of both Raamah *and* Jokshan, i.e., they become the father and mother figures. Raamah is Nabonidus, and if Jokshan is Nitocris, this union would result in "Sheba" (either as Tayma or as the Queen of …); if Jokshan is Jehudijah, this more aptly relates to Dedan, the region in which Jehudijah and her family might have originally lived (as I explain elsewhere).

The "Yok/Yak/Yek" element of these names may stem from the verb *yaqad*, meaning "to burn continuously," e.g., the sacred flame in the tabernacle, the wrath of God, or, perhaps, the unceasing anger of Nabonidus, as demonstrated in both the Song and the exodus narratives. It might even allude to the burning of the Qenite furnaces at Sinai, which, of course, would tally with the near-Tayma location and the link to Aaron and Jehudijah.

I later discovered this passage from the Midrash that complicates things a little more:

> Rami bar Yeḥezkel said: Zimran – [he was called this] because they [his descendants] would "prune [*mezamrin*]" the world [of its inhabitants]; Yokshan – because they acted with ferocity [*mitkashin*] in the world. The Rabbis said: Zimran

– because they would sing praises [*mezamrin*] in idol worship; Yokshan – because they would bang [*makshin*] on the drum for idol worship.[29]

This seems to suggest that Zimran and Jokshan are to be seen 'together', linked by music. Jokshan is "beating" a drum-like instrument. In *Arabian Sinai*, I discuss Miriam and her "timbrel" (Exod 15:20-1), which is quite a significant scene. I also discuss the death of Zimri (whom I suggest might be Aaron) and Cozbi (who is Jehudijah), in Num 25:6-15, the former being the "musician" for the latter.[30] Are the rabbis hinting that they, too, can see that "Jokshan" is a camouflaged female?

Miriam is the most obvious example of a woman in the HB beating an instrument.[31] I argue that Miriam is Aaron's wife; she is Nabonidus' daughter, Ennigaldi-Nanna. She is also Jehudijah's *biological* daughter, but in the HB, on a superficial level, she is seen as Nitocris' child (both in the Song of Solomon and 1 Chronicles 4); only by decoding the Song can we learn how this came about (i.e., the feigned pregnancy and the stolen child). If "Jokshan" is equated with Miriam, and "Zimran" is Aaron, then the etymology of "Jokshan" has to be seen as a case of "like mother like daughter," i.e., the etymology is passed on.[32] This does have a precedent in the Song, i.e., where the "little sister" of Song 8 is discussed in terms of emulating her "mother." Nitocris is not remembered for anything musical, but Jehudijah was a poet, who was accompanied by a musician, i.e., Aaron/Zimri; and Miriam and Aaron are 'musical' husband and wife.

---

[29] Bereshit Rabbah 61, The Sefaria Midrash Rabbah, 2022, www.sefaria.org.

[30] Tyson, *Arabian Sinai*, 354-8; 360-1.

[31] Tyson, *Arabian Sinai*, 30-3.

[32] But from which "mother"? Hints of Solomon's judgement again, in 1 Kgs 3:16-28, which I have claimed is about Nitocris, Jehudijah, and the 'stolen' child.

So is "Jokshan" a symbolic blend of these three women, Nitocris, Jehudijah, and Miriam? Does the character represent Nabonidus' 'women' (two wives and a daughter) in Arabia, or women in general? I think "Jokshan" *must* represent an Arabian element; although most of the suggested meanings do suit Nitocris, the main instigator of all Nabonidus' problems, we are supposed to believe, others pertain to Jehudijah and her Arabian daughter, "Miriam." Nitocris' story in the Song is set in Tayma (*not* Jerusalem, recall) and, as the "Queen of Sheba/Tayma" she was, at least temporarily, resident in Arabia.

Keturah's offspring, therefore, represent the most important elements (to the authors of the list) of Nabonidus' campaign, i.e., Aaron, the three women (Nitocris, Jehudijah, and Miriam), the beating of the rock, the dispersal of the Ishmaelites, the site of Tayma, and Belshazzar (the hero, "Joshua"). In other words, the metaphorical "children" of Keturah represent the *historical* world of Nabonidus in Arabia. Note that Sinai itself is not a direct aspect of any of these names; *that* is appropriated by the Israelites who "cross over" to Canaan.

If "Sheba and Dedan" are the 'offspring' of Raamah *and* Jokshan, this suggests the HB's account of everything within this domain, i.e., anywhere on the Mas'a (route), from Tayma to Dedan, near the Harraat, was (ultimately) the product of Nabonidus and his women. That's just what we find in the exodus narratives.

4

Hatshepsut

THERE IS A PROPOSAL THAT THE Queen of Sheba was actually the 18th Dynasty Egyptian pharaoh, Hatshepsut.[1] The argument rests on a conventional understanding "Solomon" as King of Israel in Jerusalem, on Jerusalem being Punt, and on Hatshepsut being contemporaneous with Solomon. Proponents suggest that the famous trading expedition to Punt undertaken by Hatshepsut was actually the same excursion as that recorded for the Queen of Sheba in 1 Kings.

"Solomon," I contend, was a name invented by the author of the Song of Solomon, Jehudijah, for Nabonidus.[2] There was no "King of Israel" by that name, least of all before the 6th Century BCE. The Song tells of the life and

---

[1] For a detailed analysis and refutation of this theory see Donald K. Mills, "Thutmose III, Hatshepsut, Emmet Sweeney, and the Location of Punt", Parts 1 (2021:1), 2 (2021:2), and 3 (2022:1), *Chronology and Catastrophism Review,* https://www.academia.edu/79187339/78569715/79188472.

[2] Tyson, *She Brought,* 46-7.

times of Nabonidus, ending just after the fall of Babylon in 539 BCE, so any other references to "Solomon" in the HB are to be assessed with the knowledge of what the Song says about him.

So, for scholars to repeatedly refer back to a wholly unsubstantiated entity (i.e., Solomon) with no concrete extra-biblical textual or archaeological evidence, in their efforts to explain *another* apparently unsubstantiated entity (the Queen of Sheba) seems futile. The resulting absence of knowledge on either bears witness to that. Once you are willing to leave the safety of convention and just *consider* that tradition might not always be the best route to wisdom, and you check for yourself if Nabonidus *might just be* the fundamental inspiration behind the Solomon legends (and those of Abraham and Moses), a bridge of possibilities allows you cross over from myth into real *history*.

Hatshepsut did *not* live at the same time as Solomon because "Solomon" is Nabonidus, who lived many hundreds of years later. The story of her trip to Punt might, however, have a bearing on understanding the connection between Nitocris and the Queen of Sheba story.

Firstly, and most obviously, both women were Egyptian royals. Hatshepsut was Pharaoh but she was also God's Wife; Nitocris was a princess but she was First Prophet of Amun and probably either the God's Adoratrice and/or, I have surmised, God's Hand.[3] Hatshepsut honoured her God's Wife title more than any other, to the point of making it her "sole identifying title,"[4] and Nitocris fought vehemently to retain the sanctity of her role, i.e., as the guardian of the Elixir.

More significantly, the pharaoh's famous excursion to Punt, or "God's Land," was widely heralded as a remarkable achievement (as seen in the inscriptions at her

---

[3] Tyson, *She Brought*, 10-11; 55; 124, etc.

[4] Miriam Ayad, *God's Wife, God's Servant: The God's Wife of Amun (c. 740-525 BC)* (Abingdon: Routledge, 2009), 6.

Deir el-Bahari temple) but also as a deeply personal act of honouring the Sun god, Amun-Re and the "Lady of Punt," Hathor.[5] The high priest of Karnak at that time was involved in the preparations for the trip, making it a religiously significant expedition, and Hatshepsut was directly involved with the precious goods in two very specific ways. She was so enamoured by the sacred Terraces of Myrrh, she ordered saplings of the myrrh trees to be dug up for eventual transplantation into the temple gardens of Karnak, in honour of Amun-Re. She also surrounded herself with the fragrance of myrrh, which was prized in Egyptian religious rites:

> [Her] Majesty herself was acting with her arms, putting the myrrh-unguent upon all her limbs: her smell is the divine aroma as her odour mingles with Punt and her skin glitters with electrum, shining like the stars ....[6]

Symbolically, Hatshepsut transformed herself into a living avatar of Punt; "she mingled her own royal aroma with the odour of Punt, which, as we know from other texts from the Deir el-Bahari temple, is the smell of Amun-Re himself"; thus, she is also equated with the solar deity.[7]

> *From the 13th Dynasty there is a reference to a "'boat-borne ritual,' "greatly flooded with the scent of Punt', in which King Neferhotep I presented 'myrrh, wine, and divine products' to the god Osiris."*[8]

---

[5] Filip Taterka, "Hatshepsut's Expedition to the Land of Punt: Novelty or Tradition?," *Current Research in Egyptology 2015, Proceedings of the Sixteenth Annual Symposium University of Oxford, United Kingdom 15-18 April 2015*, Christelle Alvarez, et al. eds. (Oxbow Books, 2016), 114-23, here 115.

[6] Taterka, "Hatshepsut's Expedition," 119.

[7] Taterka, "Hatshepsut's Expedition," 120.

[8] Pearce Paul Creasman, "Hatshepsut and the Politics of

The Song of Solomon is strongly imbued with the symbolism of myrrh, both as an ill omen, due to its association with death, and for its seductive qualities. The king is likened to myrrh between Nitocris' breasts (Song 1:13); it is mentioned as one of the items arriving at Tayma from the desert, i.e., from the trade route, via a caravan (3:6); it is a euphemism for the pudenda (4:6); it becomes one of the ingredients in a potion to end pregnancy (4:14); Solomon consumes it as part of an initiation ceremony into the Elixir rite (5:1); Nitocris' womb-blood is referred to as "liquid myrrh" (5:5) and Solomon's lips are described in exactly the same manner, suggesting the imbibing ritual (5:13).

The Song uses the concept of fragrance in the context of religious intoxication and reverence, but also sexuality. The Elixir Rubeus, one of the most sacred, sexual, and secretive rites that induced altered states of consciousness so that the pharaoh might experience divinity (e.g., of Amun-Re), permeates the Song of Solomon like the scent of myrrh.

Thus, on a few levels, Hatshepsut and Nitocris are comparable. Both women knew the significance of myrrh to Amun-Re, both were worshippers of the Sun god, and both immersed themselves in the aromatic resin (both physically and metaphorically). And this is where "Keturah" fits in, too, with the translation of "incense," for myrrh was the ultimate incense for Egyptian temples. The powerful imagery of Hatshepsut, enveloped in the seductive scent of myrrh, certainly echoes the mysterious Queen of Sheba coming through the desert with all her spices.

Also, there is a hint of Inanna in Hatshepsut's transplanting of the myrrh trees. The Song's depiction of Nitocris is strongly formatted on her being an avatar of

---

Punt," *African Archaeological Review* 31 (2014): 395-405, here, 397.

Inanna-Ishtar, the blood-addicted, amoral, wicked "harlot" of the exiles' vivid imagination. She, too, covered her body in scented oils.[9]

One of the most famous early tales of Inanna is called "The *Huluppu*-Tree."[10] It tells of Inanna discovering an uprooted tree on the shores of the Euphrates and bringing it back to plant in *her* "holy garden." Eventually the tree is made into a throne and a bed for the goddess, and two un-deciphered items for Gilgamesh, which may be emblems of kingship.

Just as Hatshepsut used the acquisition of the myrrh trees for Amun-Re's garden as a sign of her legitimacy as King[11] and as a devout God's Wife, so Inanna's tree is a symbol of the sacred tree in the deity's garden, but also of the potential legitimisation of Gilgamesh (whom Nabonidus emulates at times) as king of Uruk.

The Song's caravan, coming over the horizon in a cloud of dust and incense (Song 3:6) would have been reminiscent of Hatshepsut's Puntite marvels being unloaded from the vessels on the Red Sea, transported across the desert to the Nile, and arriving at Karnak. But this has a potential historical parallel pertaining to Nitocris, for in *She Brought*, I suggest that the tale of Nitetis in Herodotus' account of the marriage agreement between (allegedly) either Cambyses or Cyrus and Ahmose III (*Hist.* 3.1) is actually a misunderstood rumour concerning the conciliatory marriage of Nabonidus and Nitocris II.[12]

Nitocris was possibly the firstborn of Ahmose after

---

[9] Diane Wolkstein and Samuel Noah Kramer, *Inanna, Queen of Heaven and Earth: Her Stories and Hymns from Sumer*, (New York: Harper & Row, 1983), 35.

[10] Wolkstein and Kramer, 3-9.

[11] Taterka, "Hatshepsut's Expedition," 119.

[12] Tyson, *She Brought*, 7-13.

his seizure of the throne. She was made the first ever female high priest of Amun (First Prophet), and was an important and powerful woman at Thebes. As such, when she was to be married, she would normally have been sent to her future husband laden with many riches, as part of the marriage deal. Herodotus mentions that Ahmose sent her (i.e., as "Nitetis") away with gold and expensive garments, but had the situation been less dire and the marriage more 'normal', the goods accompanying the princess would have been phenomenal. As it was, the marriage was a matter of urgency, being the deal breaker between Egypt and Babylon during the coalition against Cyrus (549 BCE), and everything had to be done hastily and discretely.

Even the God's Wives were treated as though they were truly getting married, for they were sent to Thebes with immense riches as a sort of dowry. The Adoption Stele of the Divine Adoratrice/God's Wife, Nitocris I, describes the cavalcade that traversed great distances, awing the crowds with its grandeur. From the commemorative stele of her ritual adoption at Thebes we read:

> ... went forth his eldest daughter from the king's family apartments, clad in fine linen, and newly adorned with malachite. ... The vessels bearing her were very numerous, the crews were mighty men, and they were deeply laden [to the decks] with every good thing of the king's-palace.[13]

Nitocris II was probably invested from her home, being the pharaoh's daughter, so might not have experienced pomp and ceremony to the same degree; she was also probably denied a grand marriage caravan during

---

[13] "Adoption Stela of Nitocris, Daughter of Psamtik I," J. H. Breasted, trans., https://www.attalus.org/egypt/adoption_stela.html

a time of impending war. Nevertheless, the arrival at Tayma of the first caravan of goods from Egypt, on the occasion of the formal wedding (two years later, in 547 BCE), would have made up for all that (on a purely materialistic level).

So again, there is a running motif of Egyptian, female, royal, ostentatious, opulence that might link Hatshepsut and Nitocris on a general level.

As for the "Lady of Punt" attribution mentioned in the Punt inscriptions, it has been argued that this pertains to Hathor, whose avatars, Nut, and Wereret are also mentioned,[14] and that Hatshepsut's depiction in the inscriptions/reliefs is to be interpreted as the pharaoh emulating Hathor:

> Smell of Punt, golden skin, and reference to the stars—these are all divine, or more precisely, Hathoric attributes, which Hatshepsut takes up in order to identify herself with the goddess as the female counterpart of the sun god and the Lady of Punt. This identification was supposed to be strengthened by the double statue representing Hatshepsut in the company of Amun-Ra, in which the female ruler undoubtedly played the role of Hathor as the companion of her divine father, the creator and true ruler of Punt.
>
> ... The identity of Hatshepsut as the female counterpart of the sun god is explicitly stated in the Punt Portico inscriptions, when the Puntites

---

[14] It should be noted that because Hatshepsut's inscription mentions "Mut, Hathor, Wereret, 'Lady of Punt'" and then goes on to apply the epithet "Great in Sorcery," some understand this to be a reference to Isis. Hathor and Isis were synchronised in the New Kingdom. The allusion to the goddess' "sorcery" is another potential link between Nitocris and Hatshepsut as divine avatars, for Nitocris' magic is strongly represented in the Song of Solomon.

address her with the following words: "the female sun, who shines like the sun-disc ...."[15]

The Song of Solomon, while predominantly depicting Nitocris with allusions to Inanna-Ishtar, shifts its focus temporarily, during the most significant episodes involving the 'feigned pregnancy' and the birth of Ennigaldi-Nanna, Nabonidus' daughter, whom he dedicated to the temple of Sîn at Ur.[16] For much of Song 6-7, Nitocris' symbolic avatar is Hathor.[17]

Nitocris was also a Sun worshipper, being First Prophet of Amun (as opposed to Nabonidus' long-standing lunar preference, a dichotomy that explains quite a lot in the Song's narrative); her father, Ahmose III, was the earthly representation of Amun. This links directly to the Quran's depiction of the Queen of Sheba (27:23-5), where the emissary returns to Solomon and describes the 'heathen' of Sheba who worship the Sun.[18]

Hatshepsut's Punt expedition "appears to have been the final step in the re-establishment of past Egyptian glory – a step that was only possible after re-unification, internal stabilisation, and elimination of external enemies by Hatshepsut's direct predecessors in the 18th dynasty."[19] The same situation seems to have arisen in Ahmose' day, with a resurgence of pride in Egypt's past, once the dust had settled and his reign brought peace and prosperity. Resuming the glorious Punt expeditions was inevitable.[20]

---

[15] Filip Taterka, "Hatshepsut's Punt Reliefs: Their Structure and Function," *Journal of the American Research Center in Egypt* 55 (2019): 193-207, here, 202.

[16] Tyson, *She Brought*, 189

[17] Tyson, *She Brought*, 153-71; 201.

[18] Mustansir Mir, "The Queen of Sheba's Conversion in Q. 27:44: A Problem Examined," *Journal of Qur'anic Studies* 9.2 (2007): 43-56, here 44.

[19] Taterka, "Hatshepsut's Expedition," 120.

[20] Franziska Grathwol, et al., "Adulis and the Trans-

The link between Nitocris and Hatshepsut, via Punt, is potentially bolstered by Ahmose III's and Nabonidus' more recent involvement with the revitalisation of Punt/Ophir.

    Thus, Hatshepsut and "Sheba" are predominantly linked via Punt (historically/geographically), and symbolically, via myrrh, Amun-Re, and Hathor, which are also strongly associated with Nitocris. The Hatshepsut-Sheba argument reveals the tenacity of the Egyptian element in Solomon's legend, but it is not a 15th Century BCE female Pharaoh anachronistically transported into the 10th Century, we need to be looking at for answers, it is a 6th Century Egyptian priestess.

    Hatshepsut was a profoundly formidable example of female sovereignty, whose rich legacy has made her a role model for modern historians to cite but Nitocris was also a formidable woman in her own right, as the Song and also Herodotus suggest (*Hist.* 1.185-7); the latter describes her as the *ruler* of Babylon, a great civil engineer, and clearly thinks her of greater interest (and power?) than her husband. They both hailed from strong, Egyptian dynasties and both drew the attention of subsequent male dissenters who wished to downplay and tarnish their reputations. That is, as far as I can tell, the limit of the comparison.[21] I suggest we leave Hatshepsut in her own time and focus first on understanding "Solomon"; once that is done, everything (and everyone) else follows.

---

shipment of Baboons During Classical Antiquity," 1-21, here, 16, https://www.biorxiv.org/content/10.1101/2023.02.28.530428v1.full.pdf.

    [21] See also pg. 69 for Hatshepsut's throne name.

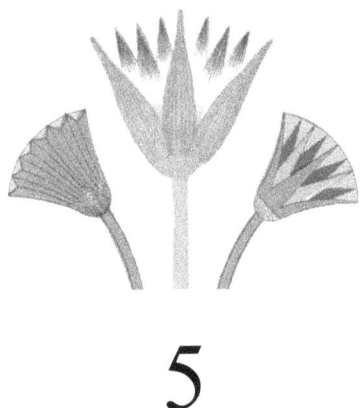

5

Ethiopia & Islam

ALTERNATIVE RENDITIONS OF THE same events, person, or place, may just contain details inherited from original sources, so must not be dismissed out of hand. Discernment is necessary when so many factions lay claim to the same past, in an effort to prove possession of lands, religious superiority, etc.

Leeman suggests that the perception of the Queen of Sheba's visit to Solomon is divided between the HB, Josephus, and the *Kebra Nagast*, which all seem to depict a positive experience, based on trade and a mutual desire for wisdom, etc., and the Jewish Targums and the Quran, which see things a little more ominously.[1] The latter, especially, reveal a sense of threat, of impending invasion, which makes the visit to Solomon a veritable peace mission for the Queen. This echoes the Song's subtle

---

[1] Bernard Leeman, *Queen of Sheba and Biblical Scholarship* (Queensland: Queensland Academic Press, 2005), 72-4.

assertion that Nitocris was 'forced' to go to Tayma as part of a peace treaty between Babylon and Egypt.

The fact that there are two main branches of the later, extra-biblical story, i.e., one from Arabia (the Quran, c. 6th Century CE), and one from Ethiopia (the *Kebra Nagast*, c. 14th Century CE), and that these reflect the two nations (barring Egypt) most linked to the biblical Nitocris, is pause for thought. This demonstrates, before a single word of the accounts is read, that a connection to the Nitocris I have been attempting to uncover with my research is plausible and consistent; she was hailed a "Cushite woman" in Numbers, she is Moses' Ethiopian bride in Josephus, and she is the Queen of Tayma, Arabia, in the Song of Solomon. That's a strong correlation to begin with.

KEBRA NAGAST

There are a few select points from the two versions that might be helpful in this quest to confirm a Nabonidus (6th Century BCE) context for the original Queen of Sheba, despite centuries of glosses. If you look carefully enough, little clues can still be seen, like minute nuggets of gold gleaming in the sunshine amidst miles of surrounding sand … in a sandstorm.

The first little nugget is a fleeting reference in Leeman's account of the *Sheba-Menelik Cycle* of the *Kebra Nagast*:

> Desirous of experiencing Solomon's wisdom first hand, the queen set out with a 797-strong camel caravan to visit him (chapters 22-24). This journey reportedly occurred in the sixth year of her reign (chapter 30) and in the seventh of Solomon's (chapter 37).[2]

---

[2] Leeman, 86. I am certain the number 797 will prove symbolically significant.

"Solomon's," i.e., Nabonidus' "seventh year" as King would have been 549 BCE. This was the year of the treaty with Ahmose III and his betrothal to Nitocris. This was the year she first arrived at Tayma with her "gold" and "fine clothes," etc., as per Herodotus' "Nitetis." The subsequent wedding caravan of Song 3 might not have been understood as a later event by the Ethiopian authors who conflated it with this first "arrival."

As for the "sixth year" of the Queen's reign, this might be interpreted as the time at which Nitocris was (so I claim) made "God's Hand." Ahmose III took the crown in 570 BCE; if Nitocris was born within the first year or so, she would be about nineteen to twenty years old at the time of the coalition/treaty. She would not have become God's Hand until she had begun menses, even though she might well have been given the title of First Prophet of Amun as a child. If this inauguration as God's Hand was six years previous to her marriage to Nabonidus, this would mean she was about twelve to thirteen at her inauguration, which sounds about right.

As I demonstrate in both my previous Nabonidus books, there are calendrical clues that have been overlooked by exegetes who simply accept convention and work within a well-defined comfort zone. There are encoded allusions to astronomical events that fit perfectly the dates within historical/archaeological inscriptions; there are allusions to historical events that can be verified, etc. Just because a precise date is not written out in black and white, doesn't mean we can't figure out an approximate date from deep within the text. Similarly, when dates or timescales *are* provided, the onus is upon the reader to find out what those dates might correspond to within the apparent context. My assessment of Solomon's timescale for the building of his house and temple, for instance, tally perfectly with the timing of Nabonidus' stay in Tayma, and subtle allusions to lunar eclipses, both in the Song and in Exodus, provide specific dates that fit the context of a Nabonidus-inspired narrative.³ The timing of the Queen of Sheba's journey to Solomon is perfect for Nitocris' arrival from Egypt, as the conciliatory bride.

In the Song, Nitocris is taken to Tayma rather hastily, presumably immediately after the treaty with Ahmose. She has a settling-in period as the king's betrothed, before the wedding. When she discovers that Nabonidus wants to get her pregnant as soon as possible, she devises a trip back to Egypt to distract him. It is this return trip, back to Tayma, that contains the wedding caravan symbolism (i.e., in the context of the *hieros gamos*). Travelling back with Nitocris' dowry (Song 3) is Nabonidus' first real experience of what Egypt has to offer in terms of luxuries, and what instigates his passion for trade, wealth, and conspicuous consumption, but also his "bromance" with Ahmose III, which becomes a major aspect of the exodus narratives. This probationary period probably would have lasted a few months, which may be the reason why the *Kebra Nagast* speaks of the Queen of Sheba staying with Solomon for "six months" before leaving to go home:

> And after she had dwelt [there] six months the queen wished to return to her own country, and she sent a message to Solomon, saying, "I desire greatly to dwell with thee, but now, for the sake of my own people, I wish to return to my own country."⁴

Nitocris *did* want to go home ... but, the dutiful daughter, she returned (to Tayma). Later, in Song 7, we learn that some

---

³ Tyson, *She Brought*, 14-16 (for Solomon's building dates); 154-7 (for the eclipses).

⁴ E. A. Wallis Budge, trans., *The Queen of Sheba and her Only Son, Menylek (Kebra Nagast)* (Cambridge, ON: In Parentheses Publications, 2000), 26.

Ethiopia & Islam

of her "own people" actually come to Tayma to demonstrate their desire for her to return to Egypt.

The *Kebra Nagast* makes it clear that the Queen was under duress to sleep with Solomon (reiterating the "forced" allusions in the early parts of the Song), who had to trick her (rather cruelly) into submission, only to be cast aside (sexually) for her handmaiden. This sounds like the Nabonidus we see in the Song.

The Ethiopian text suggests Solomon was soon making overtures regarding the possibility of a child; this is the entire basis of the first few chapters of the Song of Solomon.

> The queen then left ... taking with her a ring Solomon insisted on presenting to her as a gift for their future child.[5] The Queen of Sheba had warned Solomon that only virgins could rule in Sabaea and a pregnancy could cost her the throne.[6]

The Song tells of Nitocris' desperate measures to avoid getting pregnant, and Nabonidus' desperate measures to ensure she did. As the guardian of the sacred Elixir Rubeus, her *raison d'etre*, Nitocris had to protect her symbolic "vineyard" (her womb); as a follower of the goddess Neith, her celibacy was even more important to her. This didn't mean she would never wish to marry and

---

[5] This has a potential parallel in the "ring inside the fish" tale Herodotus attributes to a situation between Ahmose III and Polycrates of Samos (*Hist.* 3.39-43). I have argued this is one of several rumours Herodotus thought was too good to pass up but either misconstrued or simply filled in the blanks with names he was familiar with, rather than omit the tale. I think it had to do with the breakdown of the friendship between Nabonidus and Ahmose, due to something Nabonidus did, which I explain in *Arabian Sinai* (67-9). In the *Kebra Nagast*, the ring is meant to be inherited by a son (by this time, of course, the original focus on a daughter was long forgotten and replaced with a more traditional male heir).

[6] Leeman, 82.

have children but the timeframe for this unique role was limited (i.e., the purer the womb-blood, the more potent it was deemed, so a virgin source was paramount for the Egyptian rite, though when Nabonidus later exploited the Elixir, he ignored this requisite[7]). It was considered at the time that a foetus absorbed a woman's womb-blood as it grew, making the womb a less than ideal source for the Elixir. This is why Nitocris induced her own miscarriage, when she was overwhelmed by the king's advances,[8] and chose to feign a subsequent pregnancy, rather than give up her sacerdotal "throne."[9]

The *Kebra Nagast* depicts the stealing of the Ark of the Covenant, which goes something like this: Azariah, Zadok the high priest's son, forges a plan to steal the Ark from the temple and takes it and Menelek (i.e., the alleged son of Solomon and the Queen of Sheba) with him back to Ethiopia. Azariah hires a carpenter to construct a wooden box of the same dimensions and substitutes it for the Ark, without Menelek knowing until they are some distance from Jerusalem.

When Solomon discovers the loss, he is distraught:

> Meanwhile in Jerusalem King Solomon was sorrowfully reminiscing to Zadok about times past and confided to him the vision he had experienced the night he bedded the Queen of Sheba. Zadok was horrified, interpreting the vision correctly as a prediction that the Ark would be stolen and taken to Ethiopia.[10]

The Talmud states that at the moment Solomon and "Bathya" (the name given to Solomon's Egyptian bride by

---

[7] Tyson, *She Brought*, 205-10.
[8] Tyson, *She Brought*, 114-16.
[9] Tyson, *She Brought*, 133-4, et al.
[10] Leeman, 91.

the rabbis, i.e., Nitocris) consummate their marriage, an Archangel descended with a reed in his hand. He planted the reed in the sea and around it grew a thickly forested island; upon the island grew the seeds of the Roman Empire, which would eventually carry out God's revengeful plan (Avodah Zarah, 1:2, 39c). Solomon, therefore, by marrying the Egyptian princess, sowed the seeds of his own destruction and that of his kingdom.

The Queen of Sheba, Bathya, and Nitocris, are one and the same woman. Her marriage to Nabonidus was the worst moment the early Jews could imagine; they absolutely *hated* Nitocris and their loathing is palpable throughout the HB. She represented everything they had hoped to have left behind, in Babylonia; she got the blame for being a foreigner, for being a woman, for being a priestess, for holding her menses as sacred, for distracting their leader, for not bearing children, for reminding them of Ishtar, etc., etc., etc. This is why the later Jewish Targum and the Quran would turn her (by now somewhat piecemeal) memory into something that was so negative; they had the benefit of hindsight and the knowledge of what eventually happened to Jerusalem. Not so for the authors of 1 Kings 10, though they knew of the exile and what had happened on the exodus.

The stealing of the Ark scenario in the *Kebra Nagast*, I suggest, is an appropriated memory of an event depicted in Genesis 14, where "Lot" is allegedly kidnapped and Abraham sets out to retrieve him. I have interpreted this scene as a raid on the traded goods at the port of Ezion-geber, which Belshazzar had been looking after in Nabonidus' absence; Lot was not kidnapped, but *something* was.[11] Something of great value. A similar story is echoed by Xenophon, intimating Belshazzar was engaged in a fracas over goods (booty).

Might the Ethiopian authors have come to this

---

[11] Tyson, *Arabian Sinai*, 139-42.

conclusion, too, and employed the scenario to suggest it was actually the Ark that was stolen? In the Genesis story, the goods are returned, but in the *Kebra Nagast*, not only is Menelek vindicated because he is unaware of the theft until his group has left Jerusalem, but the Ark itself has been replaced by a fake, a wooden box, which means the discovery of its loss is some time later. With no one to prove otherwise, the Ethiopians declared they had both Belshazzar ("Lot") and the Ark to bring home to their land, the former becoming a forefather (as Menelek), the latter being hidden away, unseen, unverified; with no counter-claim by any other faction, it became a matter of faith, i.e., what could not be seen could not be proven *or* denied.

Perhaps more light-hearted, there is a parallel in the *Kebra Nagast* to a rabbinic tale that Solomon's Egyptian princess-bride seduced him, keeping him at her beck and call (sexually, of course) by sewing glittering gems into the canopy of the bed (Midr. Lev. Rabbah 12.5). On seeing these, Solomon would think it was still night and remain with her until she was sated.

Not only is this a reminder of the Ishtar allusions in the Song's depiction of Nitocris (i.e., as the insatiable "harlot"), it is also a reminder that Nabonidus himself was deemed to be negligent in his duties, especially in terms of attending the Akitu festival in Babylon.[12]

> Now the house of Solomon the king was illumined as by day, for in his wisdom he had made shining pearls which were like unto the sun, the moon, and stars [and had set them] in the roof of his house.[13]

In the Ethiopian 'remake' of the gem trickery, the

---

[12] Tyson, *She Brought*, 25.
[13] Budge, 30.

tables have turned, and it is Solomon who 'controls night and day' in order to spy on the Queen of Sheba.

For each legend of the Queen there is a different name for her: in 1 Kings 10 it is simply "The Queen of Sheba" but as various factions appropriated her story to suit their own agenda, the naming of this woman became a factor, when it wasn't deemed necessary originally, as "Sheba" spoke volumes within the earlier context.

In the *Kebra Nagast*, her name is "Makeda," the conferring of which is attributed, in about the 9th Century CE, to the character Azariah (the one who arranged the stealing of the Ark), and supposedly means a rather lacklustre, "not this way."[14] Later translations tend to suggest things like "excellent, beautiful," etc., which merely taps into the legend itself and the description of the queen. Many have noted that Hatshepsut's throne-name, "Makera," seems to be uncannily close to the Ethiopian "Makeda" and have used this in the aforementioned argument that the two women were the same person. The similarity is, indeed, a potential corroboration of a link between the two women, but it might simply be another example of the commission-name technique I attribute to the biblical scribes. That is, a name similar to that of the Egyptian royal name is *purposefully* applied to the "Queen of Sheba" in order to make certain allusions, such as her heritage, status, etc. Having inherited the core legend of the Queen of Sheba from the HB, which never gives her a name, the Ethiopians, being more familiar with Hatshepsut, created their powerful, independent "Makeda" along similar lines.

---

[14] Leeman, 64.

Nabonidus and the Queen of Sheba

Menelek

In *Arabian Sinai*, I mention a long-eradicated Bedouin population, hailing from Tayma and Khaybar, who claimed their decent from the ruler of Tayma' son, Buhta.[15] The ruler of Tayma was called Sulamy; the Arabic name for Solomon is Sulaimān. I have suggested this Taymanite father and son was none other than Nabonidus and Belshazzar. In Arabic, "Buhta" means "a false accusation; calumny; defamation," which may just suggest Belshazzar was, *they* thought, wrongly accused, or painted with the same brush his father had been, perhaps, and did not deserve it.

Looking again at the name given to Solomon's son in the later legends of the Queen of Sheba, we see his name is Menelek/Menelik. In Dan 5:25-6, the word *mene* is used three times in the alleged interpretation of the "writing on the wall" the king (Nabonidus) cannot comprehend.[16] Repetition is always a scribal technique to invite the reader to delve deeper. *Mene* is translated as "numbered," from *maneh*, "measure (of weight)," ultimately from *manah*, "to count, number, reckon"; but it does not necessarily have anything to do with numbers, per se, i.e., it is more a "reckoning," like saying "you are reckoned to be ..." or "he was numbered amongst the greatest ...." In context, it is a judgement of character, not material worth, hence the subsequent *tekel*, or "weighing" of the man in the context of judgment, i.e., in a definite Osirian sense, as I explain in *Arabian Sinai* (that is, the weighing of the soul in the afterlife, to reckon the deceased as 'true of voice' or not; this figures as a theme in both the Song of Solomon and the exodus narratives). I suggest that *mene* is uttered three times (like a spell), in order to remind the king (in the

---

[15] Tyson, *Arabian Sinai*, 306-7.
[16] Tyson, *She Brought*, 223-4.

context of the narrative) of his 'sins' (i.e., usurping the Tablet of Destinies, marrying the Egyptian, and becoming addicted to the Elixir[17]).

The suffix *–lek/lik* is a direct allusion to "Amalek" and the root *l'q*, which relates to "licking," especially blood.[18] I have argued that "Amalek" began as an abstract entity representing Nabonidus' co-revellers and imbibers of the Elixir, when he first lived at Tayma.[19] Daniel 1-5, written soon after the fall of Babylon, contains many clues to Nabonidus' first seven-year stint in Tayma but also hints at a few things that happened on the exodus. It is probable that the man known as "Daniel" both visited the king at Tayma and forged a close alliance with Belshazzar. Belshazzar, I have argued, returned to Tayma after Cyrus took Babylon, and became, effectively, his father's business partner.

With this in mind, and looking again at the Bedouin who claim their descent from the prince of Tayma, "Buhta," an alternative understanding comes to light for the name "Menelek," which is commonly translated as "son the of the wise man" (Solomon). Consider that Buhta and Menelek are, indeed, based on the same person, i.e., the son of Nabonidus, Belshazzar. This would then suggest that "Menelek," a name invented by the pro-Solomon Ethiopians, might mean something like "the one who was reckoned a blood-licker," like his father. As blood-rites were/are far more familiar to African religious rites than Hebrew or Arabic,[20] the inference is that the

---

[17] Tyson, *She Brought*, 5-6; 240.

[18] Tyson, *Arabian Sinai*, 174-9.

[19] Tyson, *She Brought*, 123.

[20] This remains a fascinating area of study for scholars, e.g., M. Y. Nabofa, "Blood Symbolism in African Religion," *Religious Studies* 21.3 (1985): 389-405; Luise White, "Blood Brotherhood Revisited: Kinship, Relationship, and the Body in East and Central Africa," *Africa: Journal of the International African Institute* 64.3 (1994): 359-72; Melissa Meyer, *Thicker*

Ethiopians fully accepted the blood-ritual connection and would, therefore, have seen any 'reckoning' against this practice as unfounded defamation. So in a sense, the two pro-Belshazzar groups ("descendants") *both* exonerate Belshazzar from any alleged 'sins of the father'.

Josephus

Josephus calls the Queen of Sheba, "Queen of Egypt and Ethiopia" (*Ant.* 8.6.5), which, in our discussion, fits the idea that Nitocris was an Egyptian, a royal, and has a biblical link to "Ethiopia" (and a historical one, by virtue of Egypt's control over Nubia). But he also refers to the Queen as "Nicaule," which may, as many have suggested, be an erroneous reading of "Nitocris" in Herodotus' account (*Hist.* 2.100) of the female 6th Dynasty Pharaoh, Neitakri,[21] listed in the Turin Papyrus kings list as *Ntikrti*.[22]

The only other "Nitocris" in Herodotus is the famed "Queen of Babylon," who is married to "Labynetus" (*Hist.* 1.188); Labynetus is Nabonidus, and his wife is our Nitocris II, daughter of Ahmose III. Because of the traditional reading of the tales of Solomon, i.e., as being farther in the past, Josephus made a connection between the earlier female king, rather than the later Babylonian (in fact, Taymanite) queen in Herodotus' accounts. A simple error that has cost us historians dearly over the centuries.

Than Water: The Origins of Blood as Symbol and Ritual (New York: Routledge, 2005).

[21] George Rawlinson, trans., *Herodotus: Histories* (Ware, Herts.: Wordsworth, 1996), 212, note #210 to Book Two.

[22] Percy E. Newberry, "Queen Nitocris of the Sixth Dynasty," *The Journal of Egyptian Archaeology* 29 (1943): 51-4, here 51.

ISLAM

These elements from the Islamic perception of the Queen of Sheba as "Bilqis" stand out, to me, a Nabonidus/Nitocris researcher:

✶ The story of Solomon and Bilqis begins with the king having a temper tantrum, demanding to know why one of his birds is missing and immediately becoming irate and threatening death (Quran 27:21). This is certainly an echo of Nabonidus, especially in the exodus narratives.

✶ His anger is caused by the absence of his "hoopoe," his quasi-supernatural bird (his spy, confidant, etc.), referred to in the Quran as "Hudud" (for the sound it made). Nabonidus is associated with birds on at least three occasions in the HB. From Daniel and the Song of Solomon, I discovered a thematic link between the king's enforced seven-year penance for usurping the power of the gods by (metaphorically) stealing the Tablet of Destinies, and Nabonidus' seven-year 'nightmare' at Tayma. The motif that revealed this connection was the Anzu-bird, who stole the original Tablet of Destinies from Enlil. Nabonidus erected statues of Anzu at the temples in Babylonia.[23] As Moses, Nabonidus is again linked to special birds, i.e., ibises, which supposedly kill dangerous snakes, according to Herodotus (*Hist.* 2.75-6); I have argued these were not ibis, which do not eat snakes, but peacocks, which do eat snakes and have a distinctive cry.[24] As "Solomon," Nabonidus imports peacocks from Ophir/Punt (1 Kgs 10:22; 2 Chr 9:21)[25] A very

---

[23] Verse Account of Nabonidus, i 6-7.

[24] The hoopoe's flamboyance, its crest, and its distinctive cry make it a more familiar (and 'local') cognate to the peacock.

[25] Janet Tyson, "Nabonidus, Tarshish, and Ophir" (36-9), www.academia.edu/120684427. I discuss therein a potential

interesting thing turns up if you look at the etymology of the bird commonly translated as "hoopoe" in Lev 11:19 and Deut 14:18 (NRSV). The term *dukiphath* is used in a list of "unclean" and thus inedible birds. This stems from *duk*, "to pound, beat," which the BDB compares to the Assyrian *dâku*, "kill." This is a very odd name for a bird, one would think, until you know that the peacock's Indian name, *mayūra*, means "snake killer" and one of the most often referred to signifiers for Nabonidus in the HB's related etymology (as evidenced earlier) is the beating/killing scene at the rock at Rephidim. For me, therefore, the *dukiphath* has been slipped surreptitiously into this "unclean birds" list to allude to the peacock of Nabonidus-Moses-Solomon renown. It becomes "unclean" by association with the early Jews' most despised man. It is now translated in the modern English HB as "hoopoe" probably because of this bird's association with Solomon in the Quran (27.20).

✶ In the Quran, the Queen of Sheba is simply introduced as a female ruler (27.23); subsequent commentaries suggest she was the offspring of a female *jinn* and a human king (other versions reverse the genders). From the *jinns* she inherited magic. In the Song, Nitocris uses *heka* (magic) several times.

✶ One of the main stories is about Solomon demanding to acquire the queen's "Throne" (Quran 27.38-42); he appropriates the one thing that signifies Bilqis' power, and then he taunts her with it. This is reminiscent of "Solomon" in Song 5, who demands access to the one thing that identifies Nitocris as God's Hand, i.e., the Elixir. He forces his way into her private chamber while she is performing her morning rituals and

---

new etymology for "peacocks" in the HB.

attempts to steal what he desires.²⁶ He later makes a mockery of the Elixir. In Daniel 5, the king is carousing the night before Cyrus' invasion, allegedly drinking from the Israelites' sacred vessels, stolen from the temple in Jerusalem; he makes a mockery of them, too.

✶ Solomon plans tricks to expose Bilqis, without her knowledge, to keep her in her place; one of the cruellest, perhaps, is the ploy to get her to expose her legs, which he had been told would reveal her *jinn* heritage, for demons always had hairy legs and/or animals' feet! He created a glass floor Bilqis had to walk over; when she lifted her skirts, thinking the glass to be water, the king could get a glimpse of her legs (Quran 27:44). Later authors explained that she didn't have animal-like legs but they were "hairy," so she was forced to have a depilatory treatment to remove the hair, thereby becoming the feminised, 'sex-friendly' female the king expected her to be. This is an enforced sacrifice of Bilqis' *personal* identity and power (as opposed to her sovereignty). It is much like the tale of Samson (Judg 16:17), whereby Bilqis' hair is a link to her innate supernatural powers, so it must be cut off to supress her. In another myth, Solomon spikes her food with hot spices so she becomes so thirsty she 'steals' a glass of water in the night and for this the king feels justified in forcing himself on her. There are one or two moments in the Song where Nabonidus' anger is clear, e.g., he orders the guards to physically restrain, then beat Nitocris, and he attempts to rape her, but in the exodus narratives it is his unrestrained treatment of another particular woman that heralds the end of his involvement with the "Israelites."²⁷ He goes too far.

It is clear that the Queen of Sheba myth, once a

---

[26] Tyson, *She Brought*, 127-8.
[27] Tyson, *Arabian Sinai*, 163-73.

simple tale in 1 Kings 10, became appropriated and greatly augmented by both the Ethiopian and Islamic factions to serve their own ends. One revered her memory, the other ridiculed it. One chose to see her as the mother of their people, while the other was determined to demean and denounce her. How strange that both perceptions pertain to the same person at the root of the legend.

6

Demon

THE MUSLIM SOURCES THAT REFER to the Queen of Sheba as "Bilqis" are later than the Quran, which is comparatively ambivalent about her, simply referring to her as a "ruler." "Bilqis" itself is possibly a play on the Hebrew *pilegesh*, which, as we saw earlier, suggests "concubine."[1]

With research, it becomes more and more apparent in the HB that feminine characters, concepts, etc., are gradually overwritten, wiped out, changed, so that a wholly masculine authority seems to rule the texts (though I argue for the Song of Solomon being written by a woman). Those women who do remain, fall into four main categories, i.e., the seductive prostitute/"harlot"; those who earn acceptance by performing a dangerous task or by taking on (symbolically) the role of a man (e.g.,

---

[1] Shahla Haeri, *The Unforgettable Queens of Islam: Succession, Authority, Gender* (Cambridge: Cambridge University Press, 2020), 30-1.

Deborah and Jael in Judg 4-5); the "witch"; and the "good" virgin/wife/mother. Women who once had authority are subjugated, mocked, beaten, or otherwise demeaned, such as Miriam and Jehudijah in the exodus narratives, and Huldah in 2 Kgs 22:8-20, whose importance as a 'wise woman' is negated by the etymology of her name, which means "weasel," an "unclean" animal that is reckoned "detestable" even when dead (Lev 11:41).

With a budding, strongly male-dominant Islam came further rejection of female status and power, so that the once intriguing but non-threatening female ruler in the tale of Solomon's illustrious visitor very soon became yet another example of demeaning and deriding the 'dangerous foreign woman'.

There are three animals that are traditionally associated with Bilqis, i.e., a bird (the hoopoe), the ibex (a mountain goat), and the ass/donkey. In the Song, Nitocris is described as a bird (a dove, in Song 2:14), references and allusions to mountain goats are frequent and related directly to Inanna-Ishtar iconography,[2] and the ass/donkey attribute reminds us of the comparison of Nitocris to one of the king's fine horses (Song 1:9-11).[3]

As the alleged offspring of a *jinn* and a human, Bilqis' mixed heritage resulted in a physical deformity of sorts, i.e., "either mule's feet, hairy ankles, hairy legs or all three."[4] In the original legend she had nice legs, just a bit hairy; as mentioned earlier, this hair, a symbol of the woman's unearthly powers, had to be removed in order to

---

[2] Tyson, *She Brought*, 93, 98.

[3] Ishtar, especially in her Egyptian form Astarte, was the goddess of horses and chariots.

[4] Na'eem Jeenah, "Bilqis: A Qur'ānic Model for Leadership," *Journal of Semitic Studies*, 13.1 (2004): 47-58 (here, version on https://www.academia.edu/11453396), 17.

Demon

supress those powers. Like a dog with a bone, however, both Jewish and Islamic lore gnawed away at this short narrative until it turned into something very sinister and disturbing; a nasty rumour to diminish the power of a woman over a man became an outright attack on women in a rapidly expanding patriarchal world—and, once again, poor Nitocris was the inspiration.

It was Nitocris of the Song of Solomon who became the benchmark for women in the Jewish, and later the Islamic world, whether or not she was named, noticeably alluded to, or even recognised as such. The Song, being a very early composition, set the rules for how to write about Nabonidus and his troublesome wife; it defined the difference between a faithful, loving wife/mother, and the so-called "harlot" who looked out only for herself. It lay at the root of much of Ecclesiastes and is the background to much of Nabonidus' angst in the exodus narratives. Simply thinking of her as the nameless "Egyptian bride" hardly does her justice, as her influence flavoured the Queen of Sheba myths over the following several centuries.

As Bilqis, Solomon's complex, unfathomable wife is transformed from a hated Egyptian upstart at court, into a cunning, murderous, and other-worldly demon that can make the world tremble. In an ironic twist, perhaps, she reverts to being a daunting Ishtar figure, just as she was depicted in the Song.

Ashmedai

The rabbinic tale of the king of the demons, Ashmedai (Gittin 68a-b), suggests Solomon, unable to get on with building the temple under the restriction of not being allowed to use iron tools to dress the stone, goes in search of Ashmedai, who knows the whereabouts of the *shamir*, a mystical creature, or object, that is able to cut stone on contact.⁵ The demon tricks his way into the court, steals the king's magical ring, and casts him out into the wilderness to roam for several years (cf. Daniel's warning to Nabonidus in Dan 4:19-33). In the meantime, while the king is apparently absent, Ashmedai disguised himself as the king, in order to lay with the king's women, but his favourite conquest was menstruating women, i.e., just as with Nabonidus in the Song (and the exodus narratives).

The Talmud protests a little too much, I think, when it declares that such behaviour was described only to demonstrate that Ashmedai was *not* the king. Rather a strange peccadillo to mention without any other rationale. The Song makes it perfectly clear (once you decipher it) that menstruating women were the focus of much of Nabonidus' time in Tayma. The rabbis knew this.

However, linking the 'king of the demons' to Bilqis (Nitocris) is the fact that in the rabbinic legends, it is said the women of Solomon's harem claimed Ashmedai always wore slippers, i.e., to hide his demonic, "cock's feet."⁶ With Bilqis being the daughter of a *jinn*, her grandfather being the king of the *jinn*, the parallels are clear. Bilqis, with her hairy legs *must* be as deceiving, treacherous, powerful, and dangerous, as Ashmedai. In the Song, it is Nitocris who uses her innate feminine guile and her knowledge of *heka* (Egyptian magic) to manipulate the king; it is the overall effect of her toying with his mind, allegedly, that makes him appear 'mad'.

The rabbis later invented the legend to attempt an explanation for the king's absence of mind for those first years in Tayma; they had surmised, from Eccl 1:12, that Solomon (Nabonidus) had, for at least part of his reign,

---

⁵ Tyson, *She Brought*, 28-9; here I suggest *shamir* is appropriated Shamash symbolism. After completing *Arabian Sinai*, with its strong solar-symbolism content, this makes even more sense.

⁶ Kaufmann Kohler, Louis Ginzberg, "Asmodeus, or Ashmedai," *Jewish Encyclopedia*, https://www.jewishencyclopedia.com.

relinquished power and the only way this could have happened was if a demonic force had intervened. In their minds they held an image of the demoness, Nitocris, who had inherited such powers to bring down a king.

> *Do not give your strength to women,*
> *your ways to those who destroy kings.*
> Prov 31:1-3

FEMALE DEMONS

That Josephus' "Nicaule" is the Queen of Sheba but also potentially a mistaken "Nitocris" is exciting because I am arguing for the latter two names as designations of the same person, i.e., Nitocris II. There is an argument, however, that "Nicaule" might derive from NQWLH or NQWLYS, a suggested "rendering in Hebrew or Aramaic script of two nicknames which the Greeks habitually gave to Empusa, the female demon famous for having the legs of a donkey: these nicknames were Onokole and Onokolis, 'the donkey-legged woman'."[7]

The influx of Hellenistic hybrid creatures, most of which were female, usually with both a beautiful (superficial) side, and a demonic, dangerous side, included the Gorgons, the Furies, the Harpies, the Sirens, and the Empusae. An Empusa was said to have either one leg, or one copper leg and one donkey leg, depending on the source; she was also thought to be "ass-haunched, the ass symbolizing lechery and cruelty."[8]

The Empusae were deemed to be either the children

---

[7] Fabrizio Angelo Pennacchietti, *Three Mirrors for Two Biblical Ladies: The Queen of Sheba and Susanna in the Eyes of Jews, Christians, and Muslims* (Piscataway, NJ: Gorgias Press, 2013), 88.

[8] Robert Graves, *The Greek Myths: The Complete and Definitive Edition* (London: Penguin, 2017), #55.

of Hecate, goddess of magic, or an avatar/cognate of Hecate;[9] they had the ability to shapeshift, and were thought to paralyse men in their sleep and drink their blood (and/or steal their semen). This aspect has resonance with Nitocris' reputation as the one who ran through the streets at night seeking out Solomon, who had the effect of driving him to distraction by not leaving him 'alone' at night, and as the one who brought the Elixir Rubeus to Nabonidus' court (it is just this sort of titillating, sensationalist misunderstanding that creates a legend, for Nitocris never drank the Elixir herself; her avatar in the Song being Ishtar, however, might well have fuelled this misconception, for the goddess had a fierce blood-lust).

Ishtar, of course, is often linked to, or identified with Lilith and some suggest the Empusae developed from these legends. The "Lilith" character originated in Mesopotamia, probably as Lamashtu, and would have been as familiar as Ishtar to the exiles living there. Her most defining trait was a penchant for killing unborn babies and stealing new-borns from their wet-nurses, and consuming them. She could magically induce an abortion by touching a woman's stomach seven times.[10]

Nitocris, in the Song of Solomon, induces her own abortion, using magical herbs and potions; she is hated for this and Jehudijah, the author of the Song, curses Nitocris' womb so she would never bear again.[11] The single example of Solomon's "wisdom" in the HB is in 1 Kgs 3:16-28, where two mothers come before him with one child; I have explained this as Nitocris and Jehudijah

---

[9] Christopher G. Brown, "Empousa, Dionysus and the Mysteries: Aristophanes, Frogs," *The Classical Quarterly* 41.1 (May 1991): 41-50, here 47.

[10] Jeremy Black and Anthony Green, *Gods, Demons and Symbols of Ancient Mesopotamia: An Illustrated Dictionary* (Texas: University of Texas Press, 1992), 115-16.

[11] Tyson, *She Brought*, 97.

squabbling over the child, Ennigaldi-Nanna.[12] Nitocris is the one that agrees to have the king cut the baby in half; Jehudijah, the true mother, begs to save the child at the cost of giving her up. This *is* what happens, for Ennigaldi is brought up as Nitocris' daughter (Jehudijah staying on as a wet-nurse). The aspect of the demon who steals newborns is thus also an element of the Song, for Nitocris goes in search of a female baby to 'steal'.

Figure 2: Frankfort H 1937a, "Burney Relief" (Image: British Museum);| "Lilith, a female demon of the night, has a human likeness, but she also has wings" (B. Niddah 24b)

The earliest representations of Lilith, from the 9th-7th Centuries BCE, show her with donkey's ears (linking her to the Empusa, and with the feet of the Anzu-bird, i.e.,

---

[12] Tyson, *She Brought*, 48-9; 220.

Lilith had talons, not toes, just like Ashmedai.[13]

In Kabbalah and the Zohar, the Queen of Sheba is *identified* as the non-human Lilith, having lost her humanity altogether.

The mediaeval satirical text, *The Alphabet of Ben Sira,* tells the story of Lilith fleeing from Adam because he would not accept that she was his equal. Angels were sent after her to request that she return, with the understanding that if she did not wish to return, she didn't have to. Intriguingly, the place where the angels finally caught up with Lilith was "beside the Red Sea, a region abounding in lascivious demons."[14] Why did the Jewish authors have her go to the Red Sea?[15] I say it is because they are basing the legend of Adam and Eve ... and the third party in the marriage ... on Nabonidus, Nitocris, and Jehudijah, who lived at Tayma/Sinai, not too far from the Red Sea, which becomes a central 'character' itself in the narratives (it is vital to understanding the escape route from Egypt, it is the location of Solomon's fleet, and on the other side of it sits Punt and the shores of Cush).

The author of *The Alphabet* played with the earlier

---

[13] The Rabbinic traditions become the first source of the legends of Lilith as a seducer of men and not just a child killer (Siegmund Hurwitz, *Lilith: The First Eve Historical and Psychological Aspects of the Dark Feminine* [Einsiedeln: Daimon Verlag, 2012], 63-4); she becomes more like Ishtar, the goddess they most abhorred, and the avatar of the Egyptian princess they blamed for everything from the absence of "Solomon" from his temple duties, to the fall of Israel.

[14] Robert Graves and Raphael Patai, *Hebrew Myths: Book Of Genesis* (London: Cassell, 1964), 65.

[15] Graves suggests "Lilith's flight to the Red Sea recalls the ancient Hebrew view that water attracts demons" (*Hebrew Myths*, 68); why not any other body of water? Either the Dead Sea or the Mediterranean would have been a more obvious choice for Jews in Jerusalem.

rabbis' story of the wedding night of Solomon and his Egyptian bride, and the founding of the Roman Empire (mentioned earlier), and produced a similar omen involving the same marriage, only this time with the "Queen of Sheba" epithet rather than "Pharaoh's daughter." Instead of Rome, he imagines the spawn of their union to culminate in the dreaded 6th Century BCE Nebuchadnezzar, who would then go on to destroy the temple at Jerusalem and force the Israelites into exile.

In *Arabian Sinai*, I discuss the complex relationship between these three characters in more detail than I had discovered in my first investigation into the Song of Solomon. Jehudijah, Nitocris, and Nabonidus make up a biblical trio that would have been discernible to the medieval theosophists, even without knowing of the existence of their historical counterparts for the evidence, the patterns of connection, are preserved using pseudonyms and etymology.

Moses' quasi-divine birth, for instance, and the two "midwives" of Exod 1:15, Shiphrah and Puah, form part of this overriding pattern, for these two characters are also avatars of Jehudijah and Nitocris (respectively); they are introduced this way to allude to the Egyptian divine birth of Horus and the midwives, Isis and Nephthys.[16] In a similar fashion we find Lilith later paired with another demon called "Naamah," who 'just happens' to share this name with one of Solomon's wives, i.e., the mother of Rehoboam (a fact that is mentioned twice, i.e., 1 Kgs 14:21, 31, in quick succession, indicating hidden meaning).[17] Later rabbis would argue that the two women in 1 Kgs 3:16-28, who argue concerning who was the true mother of a child, were actually Lilith and Naamah

---

[16] Tyson, *Arabian Sinai*, 245-50.

[17] For more on the biblical "Naamah," see my paper "The Three Naamahs," www.academia.edu/122986479.

(Yalqut Reubeni *ad. Gen.* 2.21; 4.8). I claim both versions of this tale (the rabbis' and mine) are correct, as both allude to Nabonidus' ("Solomon's") two wives.

After Lilith fled to the Red Sea, the angels sent to find her took it upon themselves to force her to return by threatening her with death by drowning ... "in the sea at the place where the Egyptians were destined to drown." They had begun by *requesting*, politely, with Lilith under no pressure to comply, but suddenly the mood shifts and they end up threatening her. This is precisely how I interpreted Song 7, with the Egyptian emissaries coming to Tayma to beg Nitocris to return to Egypt, i.e., when she resists, they turn nasty and threaten to expose her fake pregnancy to the king.[18] From my perspective, this is a blatant allusion to the Song of Solomon.

Why mention the watery fate of the Egyptians? This is a reference to the legendary crossing of the Red Sea (Sea of Reeds), where the Egyptians chasing Moses and his group supposedly succumbed to the deep. So why is Lilith linked to this spot? Why is she threatened with the same fate (drowning), at this precise location? Perhaps it is to underscore the Egyptian roots of the Jewish "Lilith"; she was, after all, a consequence of their contempt for the Egyptian nemesis, the "daughter of Pharaoh," who brought ruin to the court of Solomon.

Associating Lilith with the "exodus"? Surely this must be an intentional connection to "Moses"(Nabonidus) but this would be wholly anachronistic, *unless* we understand this latter-day "Lilith" to be Nitocris.

As the memory of the historical Nitocris faded, the original resentment, angst, and fear inspired by this extraordinary woman, which seems to have taken up much of the early scribes' energies, needed a substitute that

---

[18] Tyson, *She Brought*, 165-82.

satisfied a changing worldview. Peoples were intermingling, deities were adapting, but the one thing that seems never to have changed that much was the sheer dread of a woman in a situation of power, be it in the bedroom or the boardroom, so to speak. Every woman was suspect. For the early Jews, the sexual power of a woman was something to be contained, warned against, avoided at all costs save in marriage. In the Talmud sexual desire itself became a demonic force, taking on a life of its own, i.e., the *yeser*, an evil entity that ruled the souls of men. The *yeser* must (and could only) be extinguished through marriage but the rabbis warned that *all* women were sources of temptation and that *all* men could fall victim to the *yeser's* devastating power.[19]

A Note on Solomon and the Blood-demon

There is a tantalising thread of Nitocris-allusion running through the apocryphal *Testament of Solomon*, that I wish to highlight.

When Solomon, so the tale goes, meets the demons he will engage in the building of the temple, he learns there is a female demon and he asks her questions. She claims men call her "Obyzouth," which is generally understood to mean "bloodsucker."[20] When she tells the king about herself she reveals that she 1) resides in "precipices, caves, ravines," 2) takes the form of a woman to sleep with men, and her favourite disguise is that of a dark-skinned woman; 3) was "born of a voice untimely, the so-called

---

[19] Yishai Kiel, "Dynamics of Sexual Desire: Babylonian Rabbinic Culture at the Crossroads of Christian and Zoroastrian Ethics," *Journal for the Study of Judaism in the Persian, Hellenistic, and Roman Period*, 47.3 (2016): 364-410, especially 368-77.
[20] Hurwitz, 85.

echo ...."; 4) can only be contained by Solomon's power (or his angels'); this he takes as sarcasm and orders her to be beaten by his guards. And 5) she is then "sealed and bound," her power overcome, and she is set to work making hemp ropes for the temple.

When we look at these elements with Nitocris in mind, we find: 1) In the Song of Solomon, Nitocris is likened to a bird that dwells in the "clefts of the rock" (Song 2:14), which is an ominous reference;[21] 2) as the "black and beautiful" woman of the Song, Nitocris does, indeed, have dark skin, having hailed from a Libyan family; 3) the concept of being born from an echo relates to the "heavenly Bath-kol," which I mention in *She Brought*, in connection with the Elixir Rubeus and Nitocris' sacerdotal role as a seer;[22] 4) in Song 5:7, Nitocris is beaten by the guards when she oversteps the boundaries and takes it upon herself to follow the king beyond the palace. She is brought low, in a parallel "descent" to that of Ishtar into the underworld;[23] 5) this is when everything changes for her, for she becomes, as a consequence, "bound" to the new situation, i.e., she feigns a pregnancy and can no longer retain the power of being guardian of the Elixir. In effect, her power is sealed up, just as her womb had been.[24]

The "hemp rope" is undoubtedly symbolic. The *Testament* is a medieval text, and by this time rope had become a motif, or symbol of maritime travel, i.e., ships, shipping, and therefore, trade; its "its intrinsic role in both maritime industry and the colonisation and building of empire cannot be overstated."[25] Nitocris was an Egyptian

---

[21] Tyson, *She Brought*, 73-4.
[22] Tyson, *She Brought*, 96.
[23] Tyson, *She Brought*, 130-3.
[24] Tyson, *She Brought*, 133-4; 146-8.
[25] "Dancing in Time: The Ties that Bind Us" (an exhibition of a work of art made from hemp rope at the Historic Dockyard Chatham, Kent, England, 25 Mar - 17 Nov 2024),

princess, daughter of Ahmose III, the 26th Dynasty pharaoh who instigated a revival of the famed trade expeditions to Punt, i.e., Nabonidus' "Ophir."[26] Nabonidus took advantage of the newly opened sailing routes on the Red Sea when the Persians seized Egypt and completed the canal linking the Nile (and thereby Thonis-Heracleion/Naukratis) to the Red Sea (Herodotus, *Hist.* 2.158) and this allowed his trading empire to become one of the greatest in the world at that time. So, this seemingly innocent two-word reference to "hemp rope" carries a punch in the *Testament*, once again linking Solomon (Nabonidus) strongly to Egypt via his wife, Nitocris II.

The author of the *Testament of Solomon* is identifying Solomon's Egyptian wife, i.e., the woman of the Song of Solomon, as the bloodsucking Onokolis. There would have been no connection made to the historical Nitocris II or to Nabonidus, as their existence was not rediscovered for many more centuries, but this identification with the Song's leading lady goes to show that the beautiful, royal, priestly, wise, and powerful Nitocris was *still* being targeted as the 'root of all evil' that haunted not only Solomon but Israel itself, for eons.

Despite the apparently amicable meeting between Solomon and the queen, and flying in the face of the much later *Testament of Solomon*, which tells of Solomon and the Onokolis being on very good (intimate) terms during the building of the temple,[27] Palestinian amulets of the

---

https://the dockyard.co.uk/events/dancing-in-time/.

[26] Janet Tyson, "Nabonidus, Tarshish, and Ophir," 40-1, www.academia.edu/120684427.

[27] For the text see, F. C. Conybeare, "The Testament of Solomon," *The Jewish Quarterly Review* 11.1 (1898): 1-45, here, 19-20. It should be remembered that according to 2 Chr 8:11, an extended version of 1 Kgs 9:24, Solomon's Egyptian wife was not to live where the Ark had been; her residence was built away from the "City of David" for purity concerns. If

Roman era depict "a supine female devil pierced with a spear by Solomon himself depicted as a knight. This is actually the prototype of the iconography of St George and the dragon."[28] Now this is very odd indeed, and demands more attention than I can give it in this book, but in *Arabian Sinai* I argue that the slaying of Cozbi and Zimri by Phinehas (Num 25: 14-17) is an account of the murder of Jehudijah and her assumed lover … Aaron. Both are slain with a spear by a man who would go on to become the high priest.[29] This was done on Nabonidus' orders.

"Cozbi" means "false, lying," from the noun *kazab*, "a lie, falsehood, or deception." She becomes yet another wicked-female stereotype. I think somewhere along the line *someone* saw that "Solomon" was also "Moses" (i.e., based on the same real person), and all the embodied *yesers*, the Nitocrises the Cozbis of the world, were universally symbolised by the "dragon." The dragon, of course, evolved from serpent to winged serpent, to "dragon," over time; both Nitocris and Cozbi (Jehudijah) are linked to serpents, i.e., the former via her father, the

---

Solomon and 'the Onokolis' were intimate during the building of the temple, as the Testament suggests, this further affirms that the female demon is none other than the princess-bride, Nitocris, who would have been present at Tayma when the temple there was constructed, and would have had her own residence built in a separate section. Such was the case in Ur for the *entus*, who had their residence within the *temenos* but away from the temple. Nitocris in Tayma was Queen, not *entu*, but she was still a high priestess and, so the Song seems to illustrate, had her own quarters apart from the king, which would have been her right both as a princess and as a sacerdotal woman of standing, such as the God's Wives and God's Hands of Egypt.

[28] Ephraim Nissan, "The Importance of Being Hairy: A Few Remarks on the Queen of Sheba, Esau, and the Andromeda Myth," *La Ricerca Folklorica*, 70 (2015): 273-83, here 278.

[29] Tyson, *Arabian Sinai*, 352-7; 360-1.

Pharaoh, and the uraeus and various serpent-related rites and rituals, and Jehudijah because she was a member of a community that worshiped snakes as part of their religion.[30] Hecate/Empousa were often depicted with snakes for hair (like the Gorgons), and Lamia had the body of a snake. A supine female is not that far a leap from a writhing snake.

The perception of Lilith changed dramatically over the centuries, and with *The Alphabet of Ben Sira* as a foundation, medieval and Renaissance legends turned her into the serpent in Eden; where once the conniving snake was seen to be male, i.e., "Satan," now it was female, Lilith, allegedly out for revenge for being punished. The female-demon stereotype grew into a scapegoat, shifting the blame of the fall of humanity from Adam to this turbulent, seemingly ubiquitous woman.

The shapeshifting, interfering, serpentine Lilith, who entered "paradise" and changed the fate of humanity with her "dark utterances" is based on the memory of the nameless "daughter of Pharaoh," the dark stranger in the Song of Solomon, I claim is Nitocris.

So, given that Lilith is a later augmentation of the Hebrew Creation myth, we can perhaps see Adam as the easily-led, female-'controlled' Nabonidus; Eve would tally with Jehudijah, who was already at court in a relatively happy Tayma (Eden) before the foreign interloper arrived; and Lilith was "Pharaoh's daughter," Nitocris, with her apparently sinister and dangerous ways. As if to ridicule and demean Nitocris further, as the HB does incessantly, the rabbis implied that God "formed Lilith, the first woman, just as He had formed Adam, except that He used filth and sediment instead of pure

---

[30] Jehudijah was a Qenite, i.e., Jethro's daughter. The exodus narratives' serpent connections are discussed primarily in *Arabian Sinai* (274-84) but permeate several other chapters, too.

dust."[31]

Nitocris' marriage to Nabonidus was seen by the rabbis as the seeds of destruction for Israel, and in the later legends we learn that Ashmedai, the King of the Demons who temporarily usurped Solomon's kingdom, was none other than the result of the union between Adam and Lilith (Nabonidus and Nitocris).[32] Indeed, the demonic character *was* 'created' by this pair, as it was their intense, toxic relationship and esoteric secrets that led the king to a temporary insanity, which was then explained away by the Ashmedai myth.

It does make you wonder if those with the knowledge of Kabbalistic writings, or who ventured into other esoteric theosophies, found themselves face to face with the same body of 'evidence' I am attempting to explain. That is, they could see the overwhelming pattern of feminine 'blame' running through the HB, perhaps even understood the historic context of the Song of Solomon and its connection to Moses; but without knowing about Nabonidus and Nitocris, who by now were not even names in the wind, the full story could not be comprehended. They resorted to adapting the ancient legends.

Nitocris is definitely the scapegoat in the HB, in her many guises. She *is* Lilith in Paradise, and she *is* the demonic Queen of Sheba.

That one woman should be so vilified, so painstakingly woven into so many of the early Jewish writings, under so many carefully thought-out pseudonyms and symbolic representations, is astounding and just a little disturbing. Most, in the day, had probably never even seen the queen, as she had lived in Tayma, then

---

[31] Graves, *Hebrew Myths*, 65. And remember that I suggest Genesis was written after the exodus narratives.

[32] Other mediaeval legends make the two demons lovers and they create innumerable demons (*Lilim*).

was ensconced in the temple at Ur, yet it is almost as if the returning exiles felt the need to carry her ghost along with them (e.g., as "Sarah"), to remind them of the *yeser*.

Nitocris, the vilified Egyptian Queen of Tayma, became the embodiment of the dreaded *yeser*, filled with the dark magic of the female-demon sorority. Demonising the Queen of Sheba, in subsequent generations therefore, seems inevitable, as this character was inextricably rooted in the memory of "Solomon's" abhorred Egyptian bride.

It was, in some Freudian sense perhaps, a means of continually declaring the ongoing battle with the feminine forces of evil that shape-shifted through eternity, eluding

Figure 3: Hugo van der Goes, The Fall of Adam, c. 1480, Kunsthistorisches Museum, Vienna, Austria. The serpentine Lilith whispers her "dark utterances" to a seemingly already pregnant Eve; in the Song of Solomon, Nitocris goes down to the "valley" to convince Jehudijah to give her the baby

extinction (just like the masculine "Amalek"[33]). In an ironic twist, the one woman they wished to disavow through ridicule, animosity, and the removal of her name from the book of life, has become one of the most significant, most discussed, most intriguing women in the Bible, if not in history. Her identity as the bringer of the demonic is preserved as if in amber, fossilised in arcane etymology and interwoven allusions. She was the Queen of Seba, the bearer of the "cup of abominations" that, to the early Jewish mind, only the *yeser* might devise.

---

[33] Tyson, *Arabian Sinai*, 176-7.

7

Poetic License

IN LATER GENERATIONS, THE TALE of Nabonidus and Nitocris found new forms of expression, and the Queen of Sheba, that shape-shifting demon, morphed yet again. This, time, however, she became something a little different, i.e., she became a metaphor, just like Keturah.

Both Christian scripture and Arabic poetical sources co-opt, either intentionally or by osmosis, Nitocris, Queen of Sheba to serve their own ends and, in the process, consolidate the dual nature of her alleged heritage, i.e., she remains either Ethiopian or Arabian—not South Arabian but Northwestern.

With their lack of knowledge concerning historical records for the King of Babylon, and with only the Song of Solomon (relating to the Tayma years) and the exodus narratives (the postexilic years) to refer to, each side focussed on what was most important to them. For the Gospel authors, Matthew (12:42) and Luke (11:31), the queen was very much the woman of the Song, with all her negative associations and traits; for the latter-day Arabian poets, ironically perhaps, given the "Bilqis" legends, she became a romantic/esoteric muse.

QUEEN OF THE SOUTH

In both Matthew and Luke we see the "queen of the south" linked to the famous visit to Solomon in the context of acquiring wisdom; her identity cannot be mistaken for anyone other than the Queen of Sheba, so why use this alternative epithet?

Mills, who regards "the Queen of Sheba story as most likely a relatively late romance, added to such genuine history of Solomon as we possess in order further to enhance his reputation of greatness," writes:

> ... "the South" in Aramaic, the language that Jesus spoke, is ta-Yəmna'. The southernmost region of the Arabian Peninsula, where convention locates "Sheba", is named "the Yemen," the literal meaning of which in Arabic is "the South." Most literally, when Jesus named the Queen of Sheba as "Queen of the South," he was calling her (in Aramaic) "Queen of the Yemen."[1]

I respectfully disagree with the lateness of the "Queen of Sheba" legend, which I will explain later, and I have issues with this assumed translation. I do wonder why the reference to "queen of the South" in the New Testament (NT) is so often used in an attempt to understand the *original* identity of the Queen of Sheba. Not only is this many hundreds of years after the original

---

[1] Donald K. Mills, "Thutmose III, Hatshepsut, Emmet Sweeney, and the Location of Punt," Part 2, *Chronology and Catastrophism Review* 2 (2021): 3, https://www.academia.edu/78569715.

narrative in 1 Kings 10, it comes from a wholly transformed Jewish world, and from political influences that could not have been envisioned centuries earlier.

There is a general *presumption* (or blind acceptance) that the historical figure of Jesus actually spoke these words and they were not simply 'placed in his mouth' by the author of the gospel as part of a scribal technique and agendum. Also, although Aramaic was the lingua franca at the time, the *written* text should always take precedence, i.e., the gospel was a formal record and should be translated and interpreted using the extant language, i.e., the Greek. If Jesus had *said* "ta-Yəmna," why would that terminology (i.e., "Yemen") not be transcribed, if his words were deemed so significant? Why obscure such a phrase?

The more I work with etymology in the Bible, the more I notice how impeccable it is; so many commentaries, dictionaries, etc., resort to bland generalities, or even the dreaded "etymology unknown," that it becomes very difficult to figure out what might have been intended by a certain word or phrase—but not impossible, if you commit yourself to finding it out. Etymology, for my work, has been the key to unlocking great things, and I am no linguist. Yes, there is *plenty* of wordplay in the HB (and NT), but that only works when you use the extant terminology and not change it completely because a different term better fits a theory; if you need to change the original wording (as opposed to suggesting wordplay), there is something wrong with the theory.

The Greek term used in both New Testament (NT) instances of the "queen of the south" is the noun *notos*, or "south wind," and then, *by extension*, the "southern quarter/region" because that is where the wind originates. Most translators opt for the geographical "southern" first; it seems to be common sense, if "Sheba" is a location, right? I have read some rather convoluted explanations of the geographical "south" in the NT reference to the Queen, to the point of arguing over a few minutes or seconds of latitude or longitude, when the biblical authors, even the NT authors, would have known about only the degrees (if that).[2] Personally, I don't think the authors of Matthew and Luke even considered *any* of this.

"South" in the days before latitude, longitude, and magnetic compasses, for *many* generations, meant "right" or "right hand" because as one faced the rising sun, the south would be to your right. Simple.

To argue that "south" must relate to South Arabia is in conflict with the accepted nomenclature of "the east" for Arabia (e.g., Gen 25:5-6 [cf. Josephus, *Ant.* 1.12.4 and 1.15]; Jer 49:28).[3] Thus, if "east" represents Arabia, and if you are facing in this direction, "south" is to your right, i.e., Africa. From the perspective of living in Canaan, this might be anywhere from the Nile Delta to modern Ethiopia and Puntland (incorporating what we would now include as southeast). This is in keeping with Josephus' designation of the Queen of Sheba as the "Queen of Egypt and Ethiopia" (*Ant.* 8.6.5).

---

[2] The Greek astronomer Eratosthenes measured the tilt of the earth in about 240 BCE, using the angle of elevation of the sun at noon (Ravi P. Agarwal, Syamal K. Sen, *Creators of Mathematical and Computational Sciences* [Springer, 2014 https://link.springer.com/book/10.1007/978-3-319-10870-4]), 82. Longitude dates to the 3rd Century BCE, it took five hundred years for this to be applied to maps and charts (in the 2nd Century CE, by the Alexandrian astronomer Ptolemy), and it was not made accurate until the 18th Century, with the invention of the longitudinal clock by John Harrison.

[3] I checked this out on various astronomical websites that demonstrate the rotation and tilt of the earth at various times of the day, and the eastern Arabian Peninsula, relative to Jerusalem, experiences sunrise first. From the perspective of the Jewish authors, the sun rose over Arabia, which is why it retained the epithet of "the east."

The Haunting Cushite

Nitocris, of course, is Egyptian[4] but in the Song and in the reference to her being a "Cushite woman" in Numbers, she is depicted in terms of her dark skin. This is to eliminate the true connection to Libya and the Necho heritage (which would have provided her with a royal identity and thus allow her acknowledgement in the afterlife, something the early Jews did not wish to do).[5] "Ethiopia" is translated as "Land of Burnt Faces" and in the Song, of course, Nitocris enters Tayma apologising (at least superficially) for her sunburnt appearance (Song 1:6). The "Cushite woman" reference is therefore a forced association to a place known for dark-skinned people, not necessarily implying that she actually hailed from there. As Nubia (Cush) was also known for its line of black pharaohs (25th Dynasty) recall, the overall perception of "Cush" is one of 'black' and 'more-or-less Egyptian' ... just like Libya.[6] It was sufficient to carry the meaning within the context, if you already knew who was being alluded to (this scribal technique was an 'open secret', lost to later generations, and was used to depict Nabonidus also).

Josephus relates the unique tale of Moses

---

[4] To the Egyptians, the "south" represented the position of Ra at noon, and it symbolised the source of the River Nile ("The Cardinal Points," Compassipedia, The Online Compass Museum, https://compassmuseum.com).

[5] Tyson, *She Brought*, 52-3; *Arabian Sinai*, 155-60.

[6] This is a very broad statement, of course, but apart from the 22nd to 24th Dynasties of pharaohs being Libyan, they were "grouped not with the inhabitants of conquered Nubia and Palestine, but with Egypt's independent trading partners of Punt (Red Sea coast) and North Syria/Anatolia" (David O'Connor, "Egyptians and Libyans in the New Kingdom: An Interpretation," *Expedition Magazine* 29.3 [1987], Penn Museum https://www.penn.museum/sites/expedition).

conquering the Ethiopians (*Ant.* 2.10.1-2), and his conciliatory marriage to the daughter of the King of "Saba." He then goes on to claim this "Saba" is the same as Meroe (in modern Sudan), which was the southern capital of the Cushite kingdom, yet there is no other evidence to suggest Meroe was called "Saba" before the 6th century BCE (Nabonidus' day).

Note the similarities between Josephus' account and my assessment of the Nabonidus-Nitocris tale: Moses receives a princess as a conciliatory bride; she is dark-skinned; she supposedly falls in love with him 'from afar' (in the Song, it is Jehudijah's voice we hear in the love-related verses; she is duty bound to remain at a distance); there is an excursion away from Egypt, but he returns. In the alleged original version of the "Ethiopia" account by Artapanus (3rd-2nd Century BCE, Alexandria), Moses, being sent by Pharaoh to suppress the Ethiopian threat, remains abroad for ten years; this is the length of time Nabonidus dwells in Arabia prior to the fall of Babylon in 539 BCE. He went out of Babylon for ten years, then returned.

Most interestingly, however, according to Artapanus, Moses was put in charge of retrieving Merris, "daughter of Pharaoh's" body when she died. When Moses learned the pharaoh still planned to kill him, he decided to bury Merris' body at Meroe before fleeing to Arabia.[7] This screams to me of the burial of Sarah, who is, according to my investigation, Nitocris, the original "daughter of Pharaoh," and the dead "Cushite woman" haunting the Moses narratives.[8]

Meroe, a strongly Cushite state, contained a royal burial ground that lent its name to the Meroitic Period (c.

---

[7] Lawrence M. Wills, ed., trans., *Ancient Jewish Novels: An Anthology* (Oxford: Oxford University Press, 2002), 168-9.

[8] Tyson, *Arabian Sinai*, 9-13, et al.

300-350 BCE), a later phase of Cushite rule.[9]

Just for balance, even if you *were* to be pedantic and suggest a due south orientation (cartographically) for the reference to the "queen of the south" in Matthew and Luke, Jerusalem sits just about on the 35th Meridian (35.2); follow that due south (beyond the Negev) and you end up, guess where? Nubia, the biblical Ethiopia, passing to within about eighty miles or so of "Meroe," i.e., Josephus' "Saba," and *between* Saba and Punt.[10] You do not end up in Yemen.[11]

South Wind

If we then consider the "south wind" definition of *notos*,

---

[9] The British Museum, "Meroitic period of the Kingdom of Kush," in Smarthistory, March 9, 2021, https://smarthistory.org/meroitic-period-kingdom-kush/.

[10] Meroe lies at about 33.5 E; it might simply have been the most significant Ethiopian toponym Josephus knew of, which sufficed for a broad location reference.

[11] Jan Retsö claims that the mythologizing of Yemen began with Emperor Augustus and a campaign into the region in 24 BCE; he states: "Another part of this process was the location of the Queen of Sheba in Yemen - where she most likely did not originally belong - which is first documented in Christian authors, Philostorgius (4th-5th Century CE) being the main testimony for this. This mythologizing culminated in the early Islamic period when the Yemenis located a host of pre-Islamic prophets in Yemen ..." ("When Did Yemen Become 'Arabia Felix'?" *Proceedings of the Seminar for Arabian Studies* 33 (2003): 229-35, here 233. Also, *yemen* in Arabic means "south" *from* the allusion to the "right hand," just as stated earlier (in Hebrew, "right hand" is *yamin*); the right hand of what? The Kaaba, Mecca ("About Yemen," Embassy of the Republic of Yemen, https://www.yemenembassy.co.uk). So, considering this Islamic reference as a rationale for the "queen of the south" in NT times would be nonsense.

it soon becomes apparent that a potential allusion is being made here, i.e., wordplay on *notos* as the name of the Greek deity of the South Wind, "Notos."

One of the four Aurae (or Anemoi), i.e., Zephyrus (west wind / spring); Boreas (north wind / winter); Eurus (east wind / autumn); and Notos (south wind / summer), Notos was the "wet, storm-bringing wind of late summer and early autumn. *Notos dwelt in Aithiopia (Ethiopia), the southernmost realm in the geographies of myth* (emphasis mine)."[12]

Notos was known for bringing disruptive storms that damaged crops, broke up ships, and generally caused mayhem and chaos at the end of summer and into early autumn. It was often thought of as an angry, dangerous wind.

> The north wind is a satisfying wind; the south wind is harmful (?) to man.
> ETCSL 6.1.04, 11-13

> ... do not wait till the time of the new wine and autumn rain and oncoming storms with the fierce gales of Notus who accompanies the heavy autumn rain of Zeus and stirs up the sea and makes the deep dangerous.
> Hesiod, *Works and Days*[13]

> ... the south wind is harsher than all of them, ... and would destroy the entire world before it ....
> Gittin 31

It should come as no surprise, then, that the powerful

---

[12] "Notos," Theoi Greek Mythology, https://www.theoi.com/Titan/AnemosNotos.html.

[13] Hesiod. *The Homeric Hymns and Homerica*, Hugh G. Evelyn-White, trans. "Works and Days" (Cambridge, MA: Harvard University Press London, 1914), 674-5.

and tumultuous Inanna-Ishtar was also identified as being the controller of such detrimental winds, and specifically the south wind:

> He gave me the stormwind and he gave me the dust cloud
> ETCSL 4.07.6, 4-13

> She mounted on a cloud, took (?) her seat there and .... The south wind and a fearsome storm flood went before her.
> ETCSL 1.3.3 185-193

> Holy Inana embarked .... The south wind, that south wind, rose up. The evil wind, that evil wind, rose up.
> ETCSL 1.3.5, 5-13

> Riding on the south wind, you are she who has received the divine powers from the abzu.
> ETCSL 4.07.5, 5-8

If the authors of Matthew and Luke were learned men, they would have been taught of the Babylonian myths that were so significant to their forefathers, the exiles, but also Hellenistic mythology.[14] I don't think there is any reason to deny an intentional allusion to Notos, the South Wind.

In Song 4:16, the high priest Nitocris (male title retained), is about to initiate Nabonidus into the Elixir rite. She has aborted her pregnancy and has been toying with the king's mind. She is in a precarious position at this point and must win his favour again. As part of her magical preparations, she invokes the north and south

---

[14] To Romans the deity was known as "Auster," but I can't see a c. 1st Century CE tale about what Jesus supposedly said referring to Roman deities; in the context of Jesus' world at that time, the Greek allusion would be apropos.

winds:

> Awake O north wind,
> and come, O south wind!
> Blow upon my garden
> that its fragrance may be wafted abroad.

This is the NRSV translation. In the Hebrew, the last line reads: "that its spices may flow out." This is a direct reference to the womb-blood and the spices of the Elixir. She is praying to the winds to 'blow away' the remnants of the pregnancy, in order that her menstrual flow can be resumed.[15]

The Hebrew word used in Song 4:16 for "South" (wind) is *teman*. For the North (wind) is *tsaphon*.

There may be a play on Temen here, which is the name ascribed to Tayma in the Prayer of Nabonidus 4Q242 (i.e., making "queen of the south," by definition, "queen of Temen/Tayma"). The Assyrian word *temennu* means "foundation" and appears in the formal name for the famous Tower of Babel, i.e., the Etemenanki ziggurat in Babylon, or "House of the Foundation of Heaven and Earth." These two uses of *temen* (*tmn*) suggest an allusion to Nabonidus in each case; one to his life at Tayma, and one to his kingdom of Babylon. The author of the Song, of course, knows both locations, personally, and this is just the sort of wordplay she employs throughout.

The other term, for "North," *tsaphon*, is the same word used in the composite toponym "Baal-zephon," which plays such an important role in the exodus narratives. Broadly, it represents Egypt and Pharaoh Ahmose III.[16]

In the Song, Nitocris is calling upon the local "South" wind of Tayma and the "North" wind of Egypt

---

[15] Tyson, *She Brought*, 118-19.

[16] This is a complicated discussion in *Arabian Sinai*, but predominantly in 48-51; 235-8

(i.e., metaphorically/magically; she is not expecting actual winds to blow on command) to come to her aid. Both Nitocris and her Song avatar, Ishtar, are depicted as, or being in control of the "south wind." They are both renowned for bringing chaos wherever they go, with the ability to raze kingdoms at will. They were both abhorred by the early Jews.

This is a potential alternative to a geographical explanation, perhaps, for why the NT refers to the Queen of Sheba as the "queen of the south"—the authors are fully aware of this precedent in the Song and the link between the woman depicted there and the Queen of Sheba, but Matthew and Luke place this comment about her judging "this generation" in conjunction with a similar claim for the "men of Nineveh," i.e., they, too, will "judge" (the scribes and Pharisees). The point is, the queen and the "men of Nineveh" are considered the most deplorable examples of ungodly, heathen, reprobates (and Assyria is often equated with Babylon in classical texts). As the Hebrew Bible suggests both were "converted" (Nineveh by Jonah, and the Queen of Sheba by Solomon), their judgement of the current generation is all the more damning, for they have (supposedly) become veritable zealots for Judaism, and, therefore, the one "greater than Solomon" is glorified all the more.[17]

It is because of this powerful, almost destructive zealotry that the "raised" queen of the south wind makes sense; she is an imagined force of Nature, a veritable deity sweeping across the generations wreaking havoc and destroying what lays in her path. This is how Nitocris was remembered by those who could not forgive her for being who she was.

---

[17] This does have an air of Phinehas the zealot about it, i.e., the damnation of Cozbi and Zimri in Numbers 25 helps to bolster Moses' standing (at the time, and through fear).

Song of Tayma

In my book on the Song of Solomon, I discuss the legend of "Layla and Majnun" made famous by a 12th Century CE Persian poet called Nizami, and how I discovered it only after developing my own theories about the Song.[18] Basically, the legend, which is usually said to have originated in the 7th Century CE, helped to confirm much of what I had suggested the Song was about, i.e., the overwhelming passion between "Solomon" and his foreign wife that went beyond mere romance or sexual attraction; it involved mystical, esoteric rites and rituals, secret wisdom, intoxicating substances, and it was the cause of the king's alleged 'madness'.

In addition to the comparisons I presented in *She Brought*, I offer these further comparisons between the interpretation of the Song of Solomon I have proposed and the legend of Layla and Majnun:

✶ The name "Majnun" means "possessed" or "mad"; the character's infatuation with Layla drives him mad but there is a brief interlude when he seems to regain a sense of normality, only to revert to madness later. The Jewish rabbis suggested that for a while Solomon lost his mind and was 'possessed' by Ashmedai; he supposedly regained his senses after a while, but lost them again later. I claim Solomon is Nabonidus, known posthumously as the "mad" king, who seemed to lose his marbles for seven years at Tayma; he regained them temporarily while he lived back in Babylonia, but then appeared to lose them again by becoming the Abraham/Moses characters, i.e., he effectively became an Arab, with a rather strange notion for a hybrid deity, which many could not comprehend.

---

[18] Tyson, *She Brought*, 247-50.

★ The name "Qays" in Arabic means "measurement." A rather odd name to give to a romantic hero, I suggest it is actually a play on the Hebrew *mene* from Dan 5:25-6, which means "measure " (just as in "Menelek"). Nezami Ganjawi was given a commission to write a poetic narrative from, allegedly, a collection of poems, anecdotes, etc., about a mad poet and his lover. If you read the entire tale of Layla and Majnun after you have read my interpretation of the Song of Solomon you will, I am convinced, be as certain as I am that the poet simply took the Song and turned it into a more Arabic romance, perhaps to satisfy his patron, who seems not to have read the HB text. Again, it is doubtful the original, historical Nabonidus and Nitocris were remembered as individuals, but there were local legends of "Solomon" (Nabonidus) in the vicinity of Tayma[19] which might have maintained more of an Arabian flavour than the Song itself, and I think these would have inspired the poet's non-Song material.

★ There is a surprising correlation, however, between certain passages in the epic poem and the overall perception of Nabonidus, which we also see in the name given to him at Tayma, for instance, i.e., his connection to lunar worship. The poem describes Qays in terms of him emulating the Full Moon: "Two weeks after his birth the child already looked like the moon after fourteen days and his parents gave him the name of Qays."[20] Doughty, the intrepid 19th Century adventurer, was told about the ancient ruler of Tayma by some Bedouin; they called him *"Kasr Bedr Ibn Johr*, Prince of Old Tayma of the Yahud."[21] The name *Bedr*

---

[19] Tyson, *Arabian Sinai*, 306-8.
[20] Nizami Ganjavi, *The Story of Leyla And Majnun* (London: Bruno Cassirer, 1966), 15.
[21] Charles M. Doughty, *Travels In Arabia Deserta* (New York: Random House, reprint 1921 [1888]), 1.600. Tyson,

means "Full Moon." Qays is thus "reckoned" in terms of the Full Moon, echoing Nabonidus' most notable association with the lunar deity Sîn. Is this really just a coincidence?

★ Another scenario involves Qays' "powerful friend," who attempts to retrieve Layla from the grasp of her own people, who will not let her love Qays. The friend, having failed to bargain for her, and threatened with losing his relationship with Qays, says: "I shall not rest until I have sunk my steel into this stone, until I have pulled this stubborn donkey from the roof down to the ground!"[22] The "donkey" reference stands out here, as it is aimed at Layla; the best friend is not about to lose his mate to a woman! She must surely be an Onokolis, a demon, if she can drive Qays to madness.

★ There follows a strange battle against Layla's people that is basically a massacre.[23] This may be an echo of the battle against the Midianites in Numbers 31, which was against Jehudijah's people, i.e., the Qenite clans Nabonidus had 'married' into.[24]

★ Nabonidus' name is conspicuous by its absence from the HB; I explain this as an intentional embargo on his name because the Song had made it anathema. Neither he nor Nitocris are given their true names, in order to prevent them receiving any recognition in the afterlife. The poet says of Qays, when he reverts to his madness: "… they could find no trace of Majnun. It was as if his name had been erased from the book of life …."[25]

★ At one point Qays says:

Arabian Sinai, 308.
[22] Nizami, 84.
[23] Nizami, 86f.
[24] Tyson, *Arabian Sinai*, 357-8.
[25] Nizami, 91.

'Who do you think I am ? A drunkard ? A love sick fool, a slave of my senses, made senseless by desire ? Understand: I have risen above all that, I am the King of Love in majesty. My soul is purified from the darkness of lust, my longing purged of low desire, my mind freed from shame. I have broken up the teeming bazaar of the senses in my body. Love is the essence of my being. Love is fire and I am wood burned by the flame. Love has moved in and adorned the house, my Self has tied its bundle and left. You imagine that you see me, but I no longer exist: what remains, is the beloved . . . .[26]

In the Song, the king *is* a "love sick fool," "made senseless by desire"—but his desire is for the Elixir, not Nitocris. He *becomes* the "drunkard," the *saba*, because of his over-imbibing of the mind-bending potion. In fact, the name "Layla," though commonly translated as "night," has an association that matches Nitocris' in the Song, and also the notion of the "Queen of Seba" I first discussed in Chapter 1:

… Nizami plays on the Arabic word for the night – *layl* – from which the personal name Layla is derived to draw attention to the fact that Layla's tresses are a very dark black – in Arabic, *laylatun layla* is the darkest and most difficult of the nights of the month, especially, one might think, for the lonely lover. Interestingly, and certainly on theme, **the word *layla*, can also mean the onset of drunkenness and intoxication (*nashwah*) as an effect of drinking wine. *Umm Layla*, the mother of *layla*, i.e. that which intoxicates, is a phrase used to refer to the usually dark wine in Arabic.**[27]

---

[26] Nizami, 95.
[27] Alasdair Watson, "From Qays to Majnun: The Evolution of a Legend from 'Udhri Roots to Sufi Allegory," *The La Trobe Journal* 91 (2013), 35-45, here 36.

How intriguing. Not only do we get an allusion to the black hair of the woman of Song 4:1, we have a repetition of the "drunkenness/intoxication" motif *and* the link to 'dark wine', i.e., echoing the womb-blood of the Elixir! The *original* poet who devised the name clearly understood that "imbibing" (*seba*) an intoxicating substance, in an effort to achieve an altered state of consciousness and thus experience the divine, lay at the core of the Song. Nizami introduces the young couple both drinking "wine" and inhaling a "flower," probably the blue lotus, i.e., the "lily" of the Song.

In the legend we have from the 12th Century there is a complete role-reversal, whereby the lusting madman becomes a saint, raising the concept of "love" to a divine level; yet this is what we see in the Song, coming from Nitocris' character. There, it is *she* who brings to the king the idea of divine love, of the *dod* that must be earned through difficult study and initiation into secret rites by the *dodi*, the "beloved" (Nabonidus). For all the admirable restraint on Qay's behalf, Solomon in the Song is a rampant fornicator and hedonist. The Quran suggests Solomon was "always turning in repentance" (38.44), which suggests he was continuously relapsing. This echoes the Nabonidus I see in the Song *and* the exodus narratives.

★ The death, of Majnun/Qays parallels the Quran's depiction of Solomon's death. For the former, we read:

> Majnun remained as lonely in death as he had been in life. Having found his rest, he was safe from wagging tongues; for a long time no one knew, no curiosity disturbed his slumber. ... Some say that he remained lying on the grave of his love, where he had died, for a month or two. I have also heard that the time was even longer, that as much as a year passed. ... Thus the dead man was left alone; even beasts which feed on carrion did not touch him. What little remained of

him fell into dust and returned to earth; in the end nothing was left but his bones.[28]

For the latter, from the Quran:

> And when We decreed death for him, nothing showed his death to them save a creeping creature of the earth which gnawed away his staff. And when he fell the *jinn* saw clearly how, if they had known the Unseen, they would not have continued in despised toil (34.14).

In other words, both Majnun and Solomon die, unnoticed by those around them. Solomon's "staff" (iconography pertinent to Moses, rather than Solomon) is eaten by a termite until it can no longer support the dead body, and when the corpse falls the *jinn*, who had been enslaved by Solomon, suddenly realise they are emancipated from their ordeal and flee.

The tale of the intoxicating Layla and the mad Majnun is significant to understanding the Queen of Sheba legend in that it demonstrates an Arabic nuance we don't see in the HB. As I contend Nitocris II is the basis for this legend, I clearly do not support an Arabian heritage for her. She was Egyptian, through and through. Her influence over the King of Tayma, Nabonidus, however, the man that went down in local, Hijaz memory as Suleiman (Solomon), who 'built' and ruled the city,[29] was witnessed by the locals. It would have been they who heard all the scandal from the palace, they who witnessed Nitocris running through the streets at night after the king, and they who watched from below as the royal couple performed

---

[28] Nizami, 212-14.
[29] Raymond P. Dougherty, "Nabonidus in Arabia," *Journal of the American Oriental Society* 42 (1922): 305-16, here 306, note 6.

their symbolic apotheosis atop the mountain.[30] The people of Tayma claimed "Qays" as their local poet, and Nizami (who lived in the eastern Caucasus) sets his tale in the Hijaz/Najd region of Arabia.

We cannot know all the machinations of fate and circumstance that might bring together a poet and his muse but, if not Nizami, certainly the original poet seems to have appropriated the Song of Solomon for an Arabic ascetic tradition. It is said that Nizami created a genre of Arabic poetry "that dominated the literary milieu in the Hijaz for a time, then disappeared."[31] The poet must have believed the Song to be far more Arabic in nature than Hebrew, or at least as 'belonging to' Arabia by virtue of the Tayma connection (which makes me wonder how he interpreted the exodus narratives, which are even more so).

East Wind

At the beginning of Nizami's tale of Layla and Majnun, the lovers send messages to each other:

> ... he gave a message for Layla to the east wind. These were his words:
> 'East wind, be gone early in the morning, caress her hair and whisper in her ear: "One who has sacrificed everything for you, lies in the dust on his way to you. He is seeking your breath in the blowing of the wind and tells his grief to the earth. Send him a breath of air as a sign that you are thinking of him."[32]

The east wind that blows from the Najd into the

---

[30] Tyson, *She Brought*, 103-6.
[31] Salma Khadra Jayyusi, ed., *Classical Arabic Stories: An Anthology* (New York: Columbia University Press, 2010), 13.
[32] Nizami, 17.

Hijaz is called the Saba (aṣ-Ṣabā). It is traditionally considered the "Wind of the Lovers" and this seems to be a remnant of classical romantic poetry, i.e., perhaps instigated by Nizami's epic poem, in which it becomes the messenger, the bearer of all the hopes and sorrows of the lovers.[33] The Arabic word *sabwa* means "affection, desire."

I think it is a worthwhile task for researchers in this field to put away conventional boundaries and biases, and look closer at the Song of Solomon, particularly. I have suggested that the Arabic *waṣf* tradition, which is currently being debated as detectable within the Song, might actually have *begun* with the Song, for Jehudijah, its author, was an Arabian poet.[34]

It is possible that from an Arabian perspective, the Song's tale of a quest for hidden wisdom, complicated and then thwarted by obsession and madness, was the perfect foundation for a romantic tragedy. It may be due to this very poem that the Queen of Sheba legend took root in Arabia more than anywhere else and was built upon, with notions of a dramatic (and not so romantic) "love" affair, and of feminine wiles and dangers that can drive a man insane. The Song of Solomon itself provided the basis for the 'secret' child and the two female "demons" at odds with each other, etc.

So, there seems to be a literary/poetical thread running from the Song of Solomon, through the Arabian "love" poetry of the Hijaz/Najd, to the Persian, Sufi-influenced romances. What a grand world it would be if Jehudijah's inspirational and profoundly complex tale of the last king of Babylon and his Egyptian wife, at Tayma,

---

[33] For more on this topic see Jaroslav Stetkevych, *The Zephyrs of Najd: The Poetics of Nostalgia in the Classical Arabic nasībby* (Chicago: University of Chicago Press, 1993); Jokha Alharth, *The Body in Arabic Love Poetry: The 'Udhri Tradition* (Edinburgh: Edinburgh University Press, 2021).

[34] Tyson, *She Brought*, 248.

were to be recognised for its contribution to the library of wisdom *within her own land*. How generous a belated honour it would be to have Nitocris, the vilified, misunderstood, despised Egyptian wife of Nabonidus remembered as the "Queen of Saba," the East Wind that wafted over Tayma, bringing divine "Love" to those who asked for it, for this was her only goal in the Song, i.e., to share her understanding of *dod* with the man she was forced to marry.

It seems it took an Arabian mind to see beyond the biblical castigation, to delve deeper into the mysteries Nitocris brought with her, and to realise that something special was encapsulated in the Song's depiction of her, despite the negativity. Nizami discovered the *esoteric* Song (presumably from the original poet who wrote of Layla and Majnun) and perhaps this gave rise to a whole new understanding of Nabonidus' "madness." The poets saw this woman as an exotic, intoxicating, ephemeral entity and gave her the East Wind as an elegy.

Thoughts

I WAS ALREADY CONVINCED that Genesis was composed *after* the exodus narratives from my research into the Abraham/Moses mirroring technique I discuss in *Arabian Sinai*. It was only once I worked on the genealogies in Genesis that I felt my bold theory was vindicated, for the degree of exodus-related material in the etymology of those names is too great to put down to coincidence. The authors *must* have already known the filial connections, the symbolic associations, the locations, and the major elements of the story of Moses, e.g., the most obvious being the defining 'beating' of the 'rock' at Rephidim/Kadesh. Once you recognise these patterns in the genealogies, you can't ignore them; they demand explanation. Similarly, the knowledge of Nabonidus and Nitocris in Tayma, and Nabonidus' postexilic concentration on international trade hinted at in the genealogies, specifically "Sheba and Dedan" and "Ophir," requires more attention.

Most significantly for my research into Nabonidus and Nitocris, that the "Queen of Sheba" epithet can, *in any sense*, pertain to Nitocris' role in the ritual imbibing of the Elixir Rubeus is astounding. This was one of the first discoveries when I started this book, and it knocked me for six. The Elixir interpretation I expounded in *She Brought the Art of Women* must have seemed outlandish and self-indulgent at first but now, with plausible attestation in the exodus narratives *and* the analysis of the Queen of Sheba, I strongly suggest it should be an aspect of continued and serious scholarly investigation.

So why is the Queen of Sheba in 1 Kings 10 at all?

The tale of her visit sits awkwardly in the text, like an addendum, thrown into the mix as an afterthought, dividing, as it does, the account of Hiram's ships and the gold of Ophir. But what if this effect was intentional, i.e., intended for a distinct symbolic purpose? I think it has to do with an allusion discussed earlier, i.e., to "666."[1]

Nitocris the demon, the *yeser*, the existential threat to Israel from distant days, is reintroduced in 1 Kings in *direct association* with the ostentatious wealth that made Solomon a "transgressor," a leader deemed unsuitable to take Israel into the future, i.e., a direct echo of Moses in the exodus narratives. She was the one who introduced him to her "idolatry," and it was she who inspired his fascination with Egypt and its riches and metaphysical secrets. So, by sandwiching the Queen of Sheba (Nitocris, the Queen of Tayma, and the Queen of Imbibing) between two descriptions of how much treasure the king amassed, the effect is one of utter decadence perhaps, but certainly *blame* (yet again). The author is saying, effectively, "This woman was the reason we lost the idyllic Israel." Of course, 1 Kings then goes on to discuss how Solomon was a lost soul *because* of his wives, insinuating that his greed also lay at the root of his rejection by God.

The rabbis concurred:

> Apart from having married a Gentile ... the king transgressed two other biblical laws. He kept many horses, which a Jewish king ought not to do, and, what

---

[1] See discussion in Tyson, *Arabian Sinai*, 346-9.

the law holds in equal abhorrence, he amassed much silver and gold.²

The Queen of Sheba pericope is, therefore, another clever scribal technique, layering symbolic meaning that echoes the same sentiment in other parts of the HB (especially the Song and Daniel). It *belongs* there; it was not a romantic notion added at a later time. The imagery of the Queen amongst Solomon's riches, her "dark utterances" reverberating in his head, the mountain of gold growing, links together the themes of arcane wisdom, initiation, idolatry, conspicuous wealth, eminent 'friends', and the Elixir Rubeus. It is the Song of Solomon refashioned, encapsulated, for a new generation.

In sum, I suggest the Queen of Sheba *was not*:

- an unknown, mysterious entity
- a South Arabian ruler
- the mother of the king's son
- Hatshepsut
- Ethiopian
- a demon
- searching for wisdom from Solomon

She *was*:

- Nitocris II, conciliatory bride
- the woman in the Song of Solomon
- an Egyptian princess
- pregnant once (aborted) and feigned a second pregnancy; but had a "son" symbolically as her avatar, "Sarah" (i.e., "Isaac")
- the Queen of Tayma (therefore a Queen *in*

---

² Louis Ginzberg, "The Marriage of Solomon," *Legends of the Jews*, 1909. 4.5 (22). www.sefaria.org.

Arabia) and of Babylon
- ★ Libyan by descent (Ethiopian via allusion)
- ★ vilified, blamed, and cursed
- ★ a teacher *to* Solomon, sharing *her* wisdom

There is a technique in the scribal toolbox whereby the natural order of things is reversed, in order to infer some negative influence or interpretation. In the Song, for instance, the order in which Nitocris constructs her statue/poppet of Nabonidus is the opposite of the ritually defined sequence of creating a cultic statue.³ This is to suggest she is a sorceress (in context). I think a similar thing has happened to Nitocris, the Queen of Sheba, but on a grander scale. Everything she *was*, was reversed, cancelled out, and made into something she was not.

It's almost as if the postexilic Jews, the much later rabbis, and first Muslims, *all* on the extreme boundary of patriarchy and therefore irrational misogyny, simply could not allow a foreign woman, least of all one who defied male authority and expectation at every turn, any leniency or even ambivalence. She *had* to be destroyed at every level; historically, religiously, personally, mythologically gender-wise, etc.

However, despite their desire to quash her completely, to wipe her name from the book of life and thwart her journey into the afterlife, by using her example so often in their writings she lived on and on, reinvented, remembered, imbuing the HB and the legends of Arabia with her 'incense' far more than had she simply been mentioned and then ignored.

She has, inadvertently, become eternal.

---

³ Tyson, *She Brought*, 135-42.

Appendix
Genealogies and Meanings

CUSH

Seba	"imbibe": Elixir | Nitocris
Havilah	"whirling dance, pain": Rephidim-Kadesh | (Miriam)
Sabtah	"strike": Rephidim-Kadesh (Rock)
Raamah	"thunder": Arabia (Sinai) | Nabonidus Descendants: Sheba, Dedan (Trade)
Sabteca	"strike": Rephidim-Kadesh (Rock)
Nimrod	"mighty, rebel, over-bearing": Marriage (Enforced) | Links Cush (Nitocris) and Babylon (Nabonidus)

ABRAHAM & KETURAH

Zimran	"Singing, song, musician" or "prune, cut down": Aaron (Zimri)
Jokshan	"One who ensnares": Nitocris/Jehudijah/Miriam ("women")
Medan	"Strike, conflict": Rephidim-Kadesh (Rock)
Midian	"Strike, conflict": Rephidim-Kadesh (Rock)
Ishbak	"Sink, melt" or "Salvation": Tayma (manna) | Belshazzar (Joshua)
Shuah	"Sink, melt" or "Salvation": Tayma (manna) | Belshazzar (Joshua)

Bibliography

"Cardinal Points," Compassipedia, The Online Compass Museum, https://compassmuseum.com.

"Dancing in Time: The Ties that Bind Us" (an exhibition of a work of art made from hemp rope at the Historic Dockyard Chatham, Kent, England, 25 Mar - 17 Nov 2024). https://thedockyard.co.uk/events /dancing-in-time/.

"Madain Project Hajj: Pilgrimage to Mecca." https://www.britishmuseum.org/blog/hajj-pilgrimage-mecca.

"Meroitic period of the Kingdom of Kush." The British Museum. Smarthistory. March 9, 2021. https://smarthistory.org/meroitic-period-kingdom-kush/.

"Notos." Theoi Greek Mythology. https://www.theoi.com /Titan/Anemos Notos.html.

"*qṭwr.*" Comprehensive Aramaic Lexicon Project. https://cal.huc.edu.

Agarwal, Ravi P., and Syamal K. Sen. *Creators of Mathematical and Computational Sciences* (Springer, 2014), https://link.springer.com/book/10.1007/978-3-319-10870-4.

Alharth, Jokha. *The Body in Arabic Love Poetry: The 'Udhri Tradition*. Edinburgh: Edinburgh University Press, 2021.

Avtzon, Levi. "Who Was Keturah and Why Did Abraham Marry Her?" www.chabad.org.

Ayad, Miriam. *God's Wife, God's Servant: The God's Wife of Amun (c. 740–525 BC)*. Abingdon: Routledge, 2009.

Beaulieu, Paul-Alain. *The Reign of Nabonidus King of Babylon 556-539 B.C.* New Haven: Yale, University Press, 1989.

Black, Jeremy, and Anthony Green. *Gods, Demons and Symbols of Ancient Mesopotamia: An Illustrated Dictionary*. Texas: University of Texas Press, 1992.

Breasted, J. H. *Ancient Records of Egypt*. New York, 1962.

____. Translator. "Adoption Stela of Nitocris, Daughter of Psamtik I." https://www.attalus.org/egypt/adoption_stela.html.

Brown, Christopher G. "Empousa, Dionysus and the Mysteries: Aristophanes, Frogs." *The Classical Quarterly* 41.1 (May 1991): 41-50.

Budge, A. Wallis, Translator. *The Queen of Sheba and her Only Son, Menylek (Kebra Nagast*. Cambridge, ON: In Parentheses Publications, 2000.

Conybeare, F. C. "The Testament of Solomon." *The Jewish Quarterly Review* 11.1 (1898): 1-45.

Creasman, Pearce Paul. "Hatshepsut and the Politics of Punt." *African Archaeological Review* 31 (2014): 395-405.

Dougherty, Raymond P. "Nabonidus in Arabia." *Journal of the American Oriental Society* 42 (1922): 305-16.

Doughty, Charles M. *Travels In Arabia Desert.a* New York: Random House, reprint 1921 (1888).

Embassy of the Republic of Yemen. "About Yemen." https://www.yemen embassy.co.uk.

Ganjavi, Nizami. *The Story of Leyla And Majnun*. London: Bruno Cassirer, 1966.

Gigal, Antoine. "The Sphinxes of Sheba," Gigal Research, https://www.gigalresearch.com/uk/bulletins-19.php.

Ginzberg, Louis. *The Legends of the Jews*. 1909. www.sefaria.org.

Grathwol, Franziska, et al. "Adulis and the Transshipment of

Baboons During Classical Antiquity," 1-21. https://www.biorxiv.org/content/10.1101/2023.02.28.530428v1.fullpdf.

Graves, Robert. *The Greek Myths: The Complete and Definitive Edition*. London: Penguin, 2017.

———. and Raphael Patai. *Hebrew Myths: Book Of Genesis*. London: Cassell, 1964.

Haeri, Shahla. *The Unforgettable Queens of Islam: Succession, Authority, Gender*. Cambridge: Cambridge University Press, 2020.

Hesiod. *The Homeric Hymns and Homerica*. Translated by Hugh G. Evelyn-White. Cambridge, MA: Harvard University Press London, 1914.

Hirsch, Emil G., and M. Seligsohn. *Jewish Encyclopedia*. "Keturah." https://www.jewishencyclopedia.com.

Hurwitz, Siegmund. *Lilith: The First Eve Historical and Psychological Aspects of the Dark Feminine*. Einsiedeln: Daimon Verlag, 2012.

Jayyusi, Salma Khadra, Editor. *Classical Arabic Stories: An Anthology*. New York: Columbia University Press, 2010.

Jeenah, Na'eem. "Bilqis: A Qur'ānic Model for Leadership." *Journal of Semitic Studies*, 13.1 (2004): 47-58. Here, version on https://www.academia.edu/11453396.

Kadari, Tamar. "Keturah: Midrash and Aggadah." 20 March 2009. *The Shalvi/Hyman Encyclopedia of Jewish Women, Jewish Women's Archive*. https://jwa.org.

Kiel, Yishai. "Dynamics of Sexual Desire: Babylonian Rabbinic Culture at the Crossroads of Christian and Zoroastrian Ethics." *Journal for the Study of Judaism in the Persian, Hellenistic, and Roman Period*, 47.3 (2016): 364-410.

Kohler, Kaufmann, and Louis Ginzberg. "Asmodeus, or Ashmedai." *Jewish Encyclopedia*. https://www.jewishencyclopedia.com.

Kriger, Diane. *Sex Rewarded, Sex Punished: A Study of the Status of "Female Slave" in Early Jewish Law*. Boston: Academic Studies Press, 2011.

Leeman, Bernard. *Queen of Sheba and Biblical Scholarship.* Queensland: Queensland Academic Press, 2005.

Lyons, Eric. "Was Keturah Abraham's Wife or Concubine?" December 31, 2002. https://apologeticspress.org.

Mazuz, Haggai. "The Identity of the Sabians: Some Insights." Pages 233-54 in *Jewish Philosophy: Perspectives and Retrospectives.* Edited by Dov Schwartz and Raphael Jospe. Brookline, MA: Academic Studies Press, 2012.

McCurdy, J. Frederic, and Louis Ginzberg. "Agur ben Jakeh." *Jewish Encyclopedia.* https://www.jewishencyclopedia.com.

Meyer, Melissa. *Thicker Than Water: The Origins of Blood as Symbol and Ritual.* New York: Routledge, 2005.

Mills, Donald Keith. "Thutmose III, Hatshepsut, Emmet Sweeney, and the Location of Punt." Parts 1 (2021:1), 2 (2021:2), and 3 (2022:1), *Chronology and Catastrophism Review.* https://www.academia.edu/79187339/78569715/79188472.

Mir, Mustansir. "The Queen of Sheba's Conversion in Q. 27:44: A Problem Examined." *Journal of Qur'anic Studies* 9.2 (2007): 43-56.

Nabofa, M. Y. "Blood Symbolism in African Religion." *Religious Studies* 21.3 (1985): 389-405

Newberry, Percy E. "Queen Nitocris of the Sixth Dynasty." *The Journal of Egyptian Archaeology* 29 (1943): 51-4.

Nissan, Ephraim. "The Importance of Being Hairy: A Few Remarks on the Queen of Sheba, Esau, and the Andromeda Myth." *La Ricerca Folklorica*, 70 (2015): 273-83.

O'Connor, David. "Egyptians and Libyans in the New Kingdom: An Interpretation." *Expedition Magazine* 29.3 (1987). Penn Museum. https://www.penn.museum/sites/expedition.

Pennacchietti, Fabrizio Angelo. *Three Mirrors for Two Biblical Ladies: The Queen of Sheba and Susanna in the Eyes of Jews, Christians, and Muslims.* Piscataway, NJ: Gorgias Press, 2013.

Rawlinson, George, Translator. *Herodotus: Histories.* Ware, Herts.: Wordsworth, 1996.

Retsö, Jan. "When Did Yemen Become 'Arabia Felix'?" *Proceedings of the Seminar for Arabian Studies* 33 (2003): 229-35.

Ross, Heather Colyer. "The Fabric of Tradition." *Saudi Aramco World* (Sept/Oct, 1987): 21-9.

Sefaria Midrash Rabbah. 2022. www.sefaria.org.

Sjöberg, Å. W. "The Old Babylonian Eduba." Pages 159-79 in *Studies in Honor of Thorkild Jacobsen on his Seventieth Birthday June 7, 1974.* Edited by Stephen J. Lieberman. Assyriological Studies, 20. Chicago & London: University of Chicago Press, 1976.

Stetkevych, Jaroslav. *The Zephyrs of Najd: The Poetics of Nostalgia in the Classical Arabic nasībby.* Chicago: University of Chicago Press, 1993.

Stinehart, Jim. "Aramaic Names in Genesis." March 18, 2016. B-Hebrew: The Biblical Hebrew Forum. http://bhebrew.biblicalhumanities.org/viewtopic.php?t=807.

———. "Keturah: The Back Story." March 19, 2016. B-Hebrew: The Biblical Hebrew Forum, http://bhebrew.biblical humanities.org/viewtopic. php?t=807.

Tadmor, Hayim, and Shigeo Yamada. *The Royal Inscriptions of Tiglath-pileser III, (744-727 BC) and Shalmaneser V (726-722 BC), Kings of Assyria.* The Royal Inscriptions of the Neo-Assyrian Period Vol. 1. Winona Lake: Eisenbrauns, 2011.

Taterka, Filip. "Hatshepsut's Expedition to the Land of Punt: Novelty or Tradition?" Pages 114-23 in *Current Research in Egyptology 2015, Proceedings of the Sixteenth Annual Symposium University of Oxford, United Kingdom 15-18 April 2015.* Edited by Christelle Alvarez, et al. Oxbow Books, 2016.

———. "Hatshepsut's Punt Reliefs: Their Structure and Function." *Journal of the American Research Center in Egypt* 55 (2019): 193-207.

Tyson, Janet. *Arabian Sinai: Nabonidus and the Exodus.* Norwich: Pirištu Books, 2024.

———. "Nabonidus, Tarshish, and Ophir." www.academia.edu/120684427.

———. "Nabonidus and the Arabian Genealogies (Genesis 10 and 11). www.academia.edu/120828904.

———. *She Brought the Art of Women: A Song of Solomon, Nabonidus, and the Goddess.* Norwich: Pirištu Books, 2023.

Watson, Alasdair. "From Qays to Majnun: The Evolution of a Legend from 'Udhri Roots to Sufi Allegory." *The La Trobe Journal* 91 (2013), 35-45.

Weiershäuser, Frauke and J. Novotny. *The Royal Inscriptions of Amēl-Marduk (561-560 BC), Neriglissar (559-556 BC), and Nabonidus (555-539 BC), Kings of Babylon.* The Royal Inscriptions of the Neo-Babylonian Empire, Vol. 2. University Park: Eisenbrauns, 2020.

White, Luise. "Blood Brotherhood Revisited: Kinship, Relationship, and the Body in East and Central Africa." *Africa: Journal of the International African Institute* 64.3 (1994): 359-72.

Wills, Lawrence M., Editor, Translator. *Ancient Jewish Novels: An Anthology.* Oxford: Oxford University Press, 2002.

Wolkstein, Diane, and Samuel Noah Kramer. *Inanna, Queen of Heaven and Earth: Her Stories and Hymns from Sumer.* New York: Harper & Row, 1983.

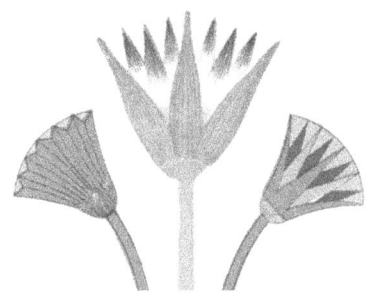

Index

35th Meridian 101
666 .... 39, 116
Aaron 18, 41, 50, 90
abortion 4, 82
Adam 91
Ahmose III 56, 59, 63, 64, 89
Akitu 68
Alphabet of Ben Sira 84
Amalek 12, 13, 19, 20, 71, 94
Amun-Re 30, 54, 55, 56
Aramaic 35, 97
Ark 66, 67, 89
Artapanus............................. 100
Ashmedai 79, 92, 106
Aurae 102
Azariah 66
Baal-zephon........................ 104
Basemath 36
Bath-kol 88
Bathya 66
beat 12, 50, 51, 115
Beer-lahai-roi.................. 21, 24
Beersheba 22, 23
Belshazzar 24, 26, 38, 40, 43, 67, 70, 71
Bered 21
Bilqis 73, 75, 77, 78, 80
birds 73
black pharaohs 2
Blackland, Redland................29
blood 3, 5, 82, 87

Buhta 70, 71
camel caravan 17, 34, 64
child 65
clothes of blue 27
concubine 32, 34, 77
Cozbi 50, 90, 105
cup of abominations 3, 94
curse 27, 82
Cush 13, 30, 44, 99
Cushite woman 9, 14, 99
dance 12
Daniel 7, 10, 14, 71
death, Majnun 110
death, Solomon 111
Dedan 17, 30
dod, dodi 110
donkey 78, 81, 83, 108
dragon 90
drunkard 5, 3, 24, 109
dukiphath 74
east wind 112, 114
Ecclesiastes 79
Eden 91
eduba 8
Egyptians 86
Elixir .. 3, 5, 6, 19, 36, 48, 55, 65, 71, 74, 82, 88, 115
Empusa 81
Ennigaldi-Nanna 9, 50, 83
Eritrea 28
Ethiopians (Moses) 100

127

Eve ... 91
exodus ... 86
Ezion-geber ... 30, 67
feet ... 80, 83
feigned pregnancy ... 27
firstborn ... 2
Frankincense Trail ... 28
Full Moon ... 107
gems ... 68
genealogies ... 1, 14, 24, 115, 119
Gilgamesh ... 56
God's Hand ... 4, 63, 74
God's Wives ... 57, 90
Gospel, Luke ... 95, 105
Gospel, Matthew ... 95, 105
Haddaj well ... 23
Hagar ... 21, 22, 23, 32, 34, 39
hail ... 21
hairy legs ... 75, 78
Hajj ... 25
harem ... 23, 36
Harran ... 7
Hathor ... 54, 58
Hatshepsut ... 29, 52, 58, 69
Havilah ... 12
hemp rope ... 88
Herodotus 19, 56, 57, 60, 65, 72, 73, 89, 125
Hijaz ... 11, 28, 111, 112, 113
Hiram of Tyre ... 10, 26, 116
hoopoe ... 73, 74, 78
Hoshea ... 43
Huldah ... 78
ibex ... 78
ibis ... 73
imbibing ... 3, 109, 115
Inanna ... 55
incense ... 28, 34, 37, 55
initiation ... 6, 8, 10, 103
ishah ... 34
Ishbak ... 42
Ishmael ... 35, 39, 42
Ishtar ... 6, 38, 88, 103, 105
Isis, Nephthys ... 85
Islam, Quran ... 73
Jakeh ... 46
Jakim ... 45
Jehudijah ... iii, 22, 23, 33, 34, 46, 50, 83, 91

Jekuthiel ... 46
Jethro ... 23
jinn ... 74, 78, 111
Jochebed ... 45
Jokim ... 45
Jokshan ... 42, 44, 48, 50
Joktan ... 30
Joktheel ... 45
Josephus ... 72, 99
Joshua ... 43
Kadesh ... 12
Kasr Bedr Ibn Johr ... 107
Kebra Nagast ... 62
ketubbah ... 36
Keturah ... 32
King of Saba ... 100
Labynetus ... 72
Lady of Punt ... 54, 58
Layla and Majnun ... 106
Layla, drunkenness ... 109
Letushim ... 17
Libya ... 2, 99
Lilith ... 82, 84, 91
Lilith, Naamah ... 85
lily ... 48, 110
longitude ... 98
madness ... 106, 108
magic ... 58, 74, 80, 82, 93, 103, 105
Makeda ... 69
Makera ... 69
manna ... 43
Mas'a ... 18, 20, 25, 47
Massa ... 20, 47
Massah, Meribah ... 13, 42, 47
Massaite ... 47
Medan ... 42
Menelek ... 66, 68, 70
Mered ... 14, 46
Merris ... 100
metaphor ... 37, 40, 95
Midian ... 42
Midianites ... 108
midwives ... 85
mighty ... 14
Miriam ... 12, 50
Moses ... 85, 86, 90, 99, 116
Muhammad ... 7
music ... 41, 50

Index

myrrh 36, 54, 55
myrrh terraces 29, 54
Naamah 85
name erased 108
Nebuchadnezzar 85
Nezami Ganjawi 107
Nicaule 72, 81
Nimrod 13, 14, 15
Nineveh 105
Nitocris. i, 23, 35, 44, 56, 62, 83, 90, 91, 93, 99, 105, 116
Nitocris I 57
Notos 102
Obyzouth 87
Onokolis 81, 89
Ophir 27, 29, 30, 60, 73, 89, 115, 116
peacocks 73
Phibionites 6
Philistine woman 10
Phineas 105
Phinehas 41, 90
pierced 90
pilegesh 34, 38, 77
Polycrates of Samos 65
priestesses 9
Proverbs 30 46
Psalm 72 26
Punt ... 25, 27, 28, 29, 30, 31, 52, 60, 73, 84, 89, 101
Qays 107
Qedarites 19
Qenite 91
Queen of Imbibing 5, 116
Queen of Seba 6, 94, 109
Queen of Tayma .. 21, 24, 62, 93, 116, 117
Queen of the Oath 24
queen of the south 96, 97, 101, 104, 105
Quran 6
Raamah 11, 17, 20, 27, 30
rebel 14
red 48
Red Sea 84, 86, 89
Rehoboam 85
Rephidim 12
Reuel 36
riddles 8

ring 65
Roman Empire 14, 67
Sabians 6
sabkha 43
Sabtah 12
Sabteca 12
Samsi 19, 21
Samson 10
Sarah ii
scapegoat 91
Scheherazade 4
seal 36
Seba 1
Sela/Petra 45
shamir 79
Shiphrah, Puah 85
Shuah 43
silver and gold 117
Sîn 4, 59
Sinai 11, 22, 51
snake 73, 74, 91
snare 44
Solomon ... 30, 39, 52, 63, 66, 68, 73, 79, 87, 90, 107, 110, 116
Sophereth 3
sorceress 118
sorcery 58
south wind 97, 101
star 6
statue 14, 58, 118
strife 42
Suleiman 111
Sun worship 59
Tablet of Destinies 71, 73
Taphath 36
Tarshish 26
Tayma 90, 112
Tayma (Sheba) 24, 27, 30
Temen 104
The *Huluppu*-Tree 56
The Testament of Solomon 87, 89
Thonis-Heracleion 26
throne 74
thunder 11
Tiglath-pileser . 18, 20, 21, 28, 47
Ur 47, 59, 90
vineyard 65
virgin 66, 78
wasf 113

wells 22	*yeser* 87, 93, 116
Wind of the Lovers 113	Zimran 41, 50
wisdom 82	Zimri 41, 50, 90, 105
writing on the wall 70	Zipporah 22, 36
Yemen 28, 96, 101	*zonah* 38

Works by Janet Tyson

Pirištu Books
Norwich

She Brought the Art of Women
A Song of Solomon, Nabonidus, and the Goddess
(2023)

Arabian Sinai
Nabonidus and the Exodus
(2024)

Nabonidus and the Queen of Sheba
Roots of a Legend
(2024)

The Testament of Lazarus
The Pre-Christian Gospel of John
(2023)

Also, academic papers on www.academia.edu

www.ingramcontent.com/pod-product-compliance
Lightning Source LLC
Chambersburg PA
CBHW061737070526
44585CB00024B/2716